MANAGEMENT INFORMATION AND COMMUNICATION SYSTEMS

Encyclopaedia of Commerce and Management Series

MANAGEMENT INFORMATION AND COMMUNICATION SYSTEMS

Edited by

Asit K. Ghosh

Prem Kumar

ANMOL PUBLICATIONS PVT. LTD.

NEW DELHI - 110 002 (INDIA)

ANMOL PUBLICATIONS PVT. LTD.
4374/4B, Ansari Road, Daryaganj
New Delhi - 110 002
Ph.: 23261597, 23278000
Visit us at: www.anmolpublications.com

Management Information and Communication Systems

ISBN 81-7041-372-9

PRINTED IN INDIA

Published by J.L. Kumar for Anmol Publications Pvt. Ltd., New Delhi - 110 002 and Printed at Mehra Offset Press, Delhi.

Preface

The flow of all varieties of information into, within and from a corporate industrial unit are of the utmost significance in the smooth management of its affairs. A modern business unit has to obtain, secure and collate outside information on product competition, marketing and promotion and then feed this information to the concerned departments to enable the company's managers, executives and supervisors to make full use of the information in performing best their various functions. The information system also includes corporate communication including in-house meetings, sales conferences, participation in sysmposia and trade fairs and exhibitions and also discussions with labour organisations as well as concerned government departments a company's corporate communication and management information system will thus be a very organised and comprehensive network for the best results.

The present compilation includes papers and articles by respective authorities and experts and will provide both students and scholars a valuable insight into the role, technique and implementation of information systems for and within the modern corporate enterprise.

Contents

1

Introduction: The Scope and Purpose of Information Systems

The main business of a corporate enterprise may be divided into six specialist functions—purchasing, production marketing, development, personnel and finance. The exercise of each of these functions involves five main activities—planning, organizing, directing, co-ordinating, and controlling. The task of managers is so to exercise these five activities that the operations of the six specialist functions are integrated in a total plan. Whilst the main divisions each have a definite function, they clearly do not operate in water-tight compartments. There must, therefore, be a synchronization of effort, involving the work of every department. Without this co-ordination it is not possible to achieve a total company objective based on totally integrated operatio s.

Principles of Co-ordination

Mary Parker Follett (1868-1933) laid down four fundamental princples upon which any enduring, smoothly-operating organization must rest:

1. Co-ordination as the reciprocal relating of all the factors in a situation.

2. Co-ordination by direct contact of the responsible people concerned.
3. Co-ordinarion in the early stages.
4. Co-dination as a continuing process.

The first principle, co-ordination as the reciprocal relating of all the factors in a situation, shows us just what this process of co-ordination actually is. On this principle Miss Follett said:

> Think for a moment what happens between the heads of departments in a business. You cannot envisage the process accurately by thinking of A as adjusting himself to B and to C and to D. A adjusts himself to B and also to a B influenced by C and to a B influenced by D and to a B influenced by A himself. Again he adjusts himself to C and also to a C influenced by B and to a C influenced by D and to a C influenced by A himself—and so on. One could work it out mathematically. This sort of reciprocal relating, this interpenetration of every part by every other part, and again by every other part as it has been permeated by all, should be the goal on all attempts at co-ordination, a goal, of course, never wholly reached.
>
> You will understand that I am simplifying when I speak of A, B, C and D adjusting themeselves to one another. They are of course at the same time adjusting themselves to every other factor in the situation. Or it would be more accurate to say that all the factors in the situation are going through this process of reciprocal relating.
>
> ---
>
> If anyone finds principle difficult to accept, I would suggest that it is a principle which he has already accepted in regard to facts. Any fact gains its significance through its relation to all the other facts pertaining to the situation. For instance, if you have increased sales, you are not too pleased until you find out whether there has been an increased sales cost. If there has been, or one out of proportion to sales,

your satisfaction disappears. Merchandising shows you this principle at work. For merchandising is not merely a bringing together of designing, engineering, manufacturing and sales departments, it is these in their total relativity.

For the second principle Miss Follett had in mind crossrelatnojs between heads of departments instead of up and down the line through the chief executive. This seems sensible as these are the people closest to the matter in hand and it is essential for them to have the opportunity for direct contact.

The third principle means that the direct contact must begin in the earliest stages of the process—writing on this she said:

> We see how this works in the correlation of policies in a business. If the heads of departments confront each other with finished policies, agreement will be found difficult. Of course they then begin to "play politics," or that is often the tendency. But if these heads meet while they are forming their policies, meet and discuss the questions involved, a successful correlation is far more likely to be reached. Their thinking has not become crystallized. They can still modify one another. I should say that one of the fundamental ideas for business management is that the making of decisions and the correlating of decisions should be one process. You cannot, with the greatest degree of success for your undertaking, make policy forming and policy adjusting two separate processes. Policy adjusting cannot begin after the separate policies have been completed.

Continuing her elaboration of this principle Miss Follett stressed that the process of reciprocal relating, the interpenetration of every part by every other part, means that departmental policy should be an integral part of what is known as "general policy." She added:

> Before I leave this point, let me call particularly to your attention that this reciprocal relating; co-ordinating, unify-

ing, is a process which does not require sacrifice on the part of the individual. The fallacy that the individual must give up his individuality for the sake of the whole is one of the most pervasive, the most insidious, fallacies I know. It crops up again and again in one place after another. In some of the businesses I have studied, I have been told that the head of a department should subordinate the good of his department to the good of the whole undertaking. But of course he should do no such thing. His departmental point of view is needed in the whole. It must indeed be reconciled with all the other points of view in the business, but it must not be abandoned.

The fourth principle, co-ordination as continuing process, needs little comment. Clearly co-ordination should be a continuous process. It must go on all the time and not just on special occasions or when difficulties arise. If, for example, an ad hoc committee is set up to consider a special problem the tendency is naturally to think only of the question under discussion. But the cross-relations referred to abave envisage continuing contacts in which not only immediate problems will be discussed but also the underlying principles which can serve as guides for future similar cases. In other words, there will always be an attempt to solve the immediate problem and an attempt to establish principles to help the collective effort in the future.

Henri Fayol suggested that in a well co-ordinated enterprise the following can be observed:

1. Each department wprks in harmony with the rest. Stores knows what has to be supplied and at what time; Production knows its target; Maintenance keeps equipment and tools in good order; Finance procures necesssary funds; and all these activities are carried out in sure, orderly fashion.
2. In each department divisions and subdivisions are precisely informed as to the share they must take in

the communal task and the reciprocal aid they are to afford one another.

3. The working schedule of the various departments and sub-divisions thereof is constantly attuned to changing circumstances.

Effective Communications

The integration of the main specialist functions in a total plan involves co-ordination, and effective commnnications play an important part in this.

Good communication depend on clear thinking. You must first know to whom and what you want to communicate, and then decide on the best means of doing it. Sometimes cricumstances will dictate the medium to be used, but often you have a choice, in which case you will be guided by one or a combination of the followlng considerations:

1. The time factor—is speed vital?
2. The accessibility of the person to be contacted.
3. Your knowledge of the person concerned: personal habits and inclinations.
4. The psychological aspect of the situation—the spoken word may be less dangerous than the same thing in writing, for example.

A wrong decision about what is said, the medium used, or when it is said can have disastrous results. All are important It's not only what you say, but how you say it, and when you say it.

Whatever method is used it is important to keep in mind at all times that communication is a two-way process. Not only is there the act of sending, but also one of receiving. Communication is not complete until there is understanding and acceptance of the message, and until action results therefrom. There are many barriers to understanding. A communication can mean entirely different things, depending upon the personal background and experience of the people involved. The receiver of a communication tends to evaluate what he hears and sees in terms of his own experience, viewpoint and emotions, with the result that an accurate exchange of ideas is difficult to accomplish.

Since communication is a two-way process we must always have the receiver in mind when speaking or writing. When speaking to a child we use words that the child can understand. We do not want to treat an adult as a child, but still we must choose our language with the receiver in mind. Scientists and technicians and business men often fail to realize this. The scientist, for example, can and does make contact with his colleagues in the special vocabulary surrounding their scientific work. But outside their own department communication is much more difficult, and much more thought is necessary to convey a message. As far as possible, unfamiliar terminology must be avoided. It has been truly said that if a person really knows his subject he will discourse on it in simple, everyday terms; to the extent to which he does not know it he will take refuge in technical terminology.

The ability to impart information clearly, completely and precisely depends on these basic qualities—concentration, discrimination, and expression. It is only when we are called upon to write or speak on a subject that we realize how vague and woolly our thoughts can be. Considerable concentration is needed to put our nebulous ideas into words and to exercise our powers of discrimination and expression.

The test of good style in any communication is: Does it do its job? Is it effective as a method of conveying exactly an idea from one mind to another and, at the same time, establishing a personal relationship with the other person?

Instructions and Employee Information

Clearly a communication addressed to a large number of people presents more problems than one addressed to a single Individual. It has been shown by many investigators that despite the many millions spent on education a large number of people go through life without really learning to read. Many can read haltingly, if they must, but they do not have enough skill to enjoy it and shun it if they can. They would rather look at pictures.

In the past official documents have not helped to overcome this weakness. Many have been so verbose that even well-educated people could not understand them. Fortunately in recent years there has been a move towards plainness and clarity in official communications. All whose duty it is to issue instructions must learn to write and speak so that the people concerned understand them, or better still, cannot misunderstand them. They must also be able to convey accurate information without ambiguity or resentment.

Orders and instructions should alway be accompanied by enough information about the the policy behind them. Over-familiarity with the subject-matter is often the cause of misunderstanding. It is easy to forget that the other man does not know all that you do. Ideally the information passed on should relate to the scope and responsibility of its recipient.

Announcements made to convey information to employees should contain statements of fact with sufficient explanation to enable the facts to be understood. The main point to keep in mind is that the writer is not showing off his own ability or status, but presenting information for others to absorb easily.

One is surprised at the number of executives who complain of "going to a lot of trouble to keep staff informed, but they simply don't read the information sent to them." When one sees some of the written information given to emplopees, one is no longer surprised; certainly nobody would want to read it. The writer should confine himself as far as possible to words that are in common use, and use the shortest word which expresses the meaning. Guiding rules are: Do not use a phrase to express a meaning which can be conveyed by a single preposition. Avoid the use of woolly abstract nouns whenever possible. Keep sentences as short as possible, preferably eight to eighteen words long, and limit them to one main thought. Remember that always the reader will want to know: "How does this affect me?"

In an official report on communications in industry, published under the title People at Work, a summary was made of the general attitudes to communications in the firms where surveys were carried out. The managers of nearly all the firms visited believed that good communications would give employees a better understanding of their work and of factors which might affect it, and would help employees to work intelligently and efficiently and to accept the need for change when it arose, Most of them also held that there was value in letting employees know what was going on in the firm generally and that in the absence of facts, rumours, often unfounded, would take their place. Again managers were anxious to know what employees thought about the firm and the way it was run, so that they could take this into account in shaping their plans and policies. In all the firms, it was felt that the problems of establishing and maintaining good communications were considerable.

For their part, employees felt that they should have clear and definite information on matters necessary for carrying out their jobs. Employees also attached importance to arrangements for raising and discussing with the managers matters affecting their jobs and working conditions, and also the general running of the firm.

Discussing the background factors the report said that there were common features in the communications arrangements in all the firms visited. There were also significant differences —for example, in the range and amount of information communicated, the methods used and the extent to which exchange of views between managers and employees was encouraged and took place. In some measure these variations were due to background factors, such as the size and sturcture of the firm, the way in which work was organized and the quality of the relationships which had been built up over the years.

In a large engineering works employing thousands of men on noisy production lines moving at a set pace, there were physical problems of communication which did not exist in a smaller firm with a few hundred employees working under one roof, each at his own speed, on relatively quiet operations.

A nationalized industry with widely dispersed units had consciously tackled its communications problems by developing an extensive network of committees and by making wide use of written mateiral. On the other hand, a small compact firm was able to rely on frequent informal day-to-day contacts between managers, supervisors and men.

Shift working may be a source of difficulty, since workers on shifts may have little opportuntiy for contact with managers, supervisors and their own representatives. These difficulties existed but were not found to be acute at factories where the shifts rotated. They were serious in one firm where there was a permanent night shift.

Whether or not a firm has a history of steady demand for its products and of stable employment was also found to be an important factor. At one factory, where there had been a constantly high level of activity for years, and employees felt that their jobs were secure, critical situations in which the directors had to take urgent action to explain to the employees what was happening were unknown. At another factory, which was subject to substantial fluctuations in activity and employment, the directors had to be constantly prepared to deal with rumours of short-time working or redundancy.

In all the firms, three main methods of communication were used. On some matters, managers and supervisors talked with shop floor employees individually or collectively. For others, written material was used. On yet other matters, information was given to, and views were exchanged with, employee representatives, either at meetings of joint committees, or in the course of informal day-to-day contacts. The emphasis placed on each of these methods varied from firm to firm.

The first method—where managers and supervisors communicate with shop floor employees—is widely used, but where there are many intermediaries not only is the transmission of information slowed down but there is an increased risk of inaccuracies and misunderstandings creeping in. The personal factor often presents a difficulty, and there is frequently a reluctance to pass on information. Sometimes this arises because a man thinks that his status is enhanced by knowing more than his subordinates. Where written material is used this usually takes the form of handbooks, notices posted on works notice boards, and works' magazines. Notice boards are, in fact, widely used, but all too often they are disregarded unless care is taken in siting and display, and in making sure that "dead" material is regularly removed. An increasing use is made of joint committees as a means of communication between managers and the main body of employees. Such committees serve as a channel of communication in both directions.

There is no doubt that accepted channels of communication reduce the scope for rumour and misunderstanding. It is difficult to eliminate altogether the "grapevine," but where there is a definite plan for communication with employees, the effect of the unofficial communications network is reduced to a minimum.

Suggestion Schemes

Employee information is not limited to information passing down the line from the top to the bottom. Much valuable information can pass upwards. Although upward communication is less frequent, a manager should tap the full resources of subordinates by encouraging creative thought and full expression of ideas, without making hasty judgements as to their worth.

Communications going downward are highly directive and initiate actions by subordinates. Communications going upward, however, report results or give information and make suggestions.

Some business run suggestion schemes to arouse the interest of the staff in the conduct of the business and to encourage them to co-operate by submitting practical suggestions. A suggestion scheme gives the worker some measure of initiative and makes him feel that he can participate in improving the efficiency and general well-being of the business.

To be continuously successful a suggestion scheme must be supported at all levels. It must be carefully planned and fully explained to the employees from the beginning. It is important in maintaining the employees' faith in scheme that they should be advised speedily and clearly of the decisions which have been reached, and that there should be speedy payment of any monetary award.

Communication for Managerial Effectiveness*

The complexity of modern organisations imposes a heavy burden on proper communication for improving organisational effectiveness. Communication includes the individual communication processes, expanding through the two-person relationships to groups and finally to the total organisational level. Vastness

*By P.K. Basu.

in size and the technological sophistication of the organisations add to the complexity of communication. The everchanging pressures of environment make their demands on organisations and through them on communication. Similarly the aspirations of the persons who work in these organisations can no longer be taken for granted. It is these dimensions which make commnication the critical factor in modern organisations.

Traditionally, it is customary to look at communications only from the behaviourial angle. In this scheme great emphasis is laid on vertical and horizontal communication. In the vertical communication process various factors like the physical distance in the hierarchy, the psychological distance in terms of background, aspirations, appreciation knowledge etc. play a part. While communicating to peers, the differences in terms of perspective and inter-personnel factors like rivalry, status etc., come into play. Some communication difficulties in both the vertical and horizontal contexts also arise due to inexactitude of language and the ineffectiveness of conveying a message.

Communication for improving managerial effectiveness, however, needs to be looked at from a wider perspective. The behaviourial and the organisational aspects are, no doubt, extremely important. They impinge on each other and have a strong influence on each other. While discussing in terms of the organisational aspects of communication for improving managerial effectiveness it is necessary also to dwell wherever necessary on the behaviourial aspects. Today, we may have to look at the subject from an even wider perspective of not only the internal environment but also external factors which have an influence on the organisation and its employees. Unless we view communication as a total concept we might miss many important essentials.

Let us examine the issue in the context of the environment that surrounds organisations. It is a good way look at the environmental factors from the stand-point of the various stakeholders, *e.g.*, the State, the shareholders or the owners, the public or the consumers, the future generation—not forgetting either the environment at home or the international influences abroad. In the case of public enterprises, the State as the owners and the public both as the consumer as well as the owner are important agents with whom communication is critical. It is not proposed to discuss in detail in this paper the issues on communication with each of these factors as stake-holders or the publics or even environment as that would require separate treatment altogether. But it is necessary to underline the concerns these various stake-holders have and the pressures that they exert on the organisations and the individuals working in it. These have to be borne in mind in any discussion of organisational and individual effectiveness.

One of the important instruments devised by modern organisations to improve communication and organisational effectiveness is corporate planning. This lession from the world of business and the State-directed economics has been widely applied by the developing countries in their efforts to accelerate economic development and growth. National Planning today in the developing countries is perhaps as common and seriously taken as is corporate planning by the progressive business enterprises of the countries of the West of State level planning in the centrally planned economics.

There are several dimensions of the impact that planning at the organisational level provides for improving efficiency. The first req irement for any progress is to have a sense of direction. This sense of direction can develop only through the discipline of planning. Planning, as we are aware, helps us to see the direction in which an organisation has to move if it has to survive and grow. In this process, we are able to set our objectives. The exercise of setting organisational objectives has a tremendous effect o1 communication within the organisation. Identification of organisational objectives also assist in the identification of strategies required to achieve them. This further improves the understanding of the organisation and its requirements by all those who are involved in it.

Corporate or organisational planning, therefore, is a very powerful tool of improving managerial effectiveness through better communication. In our country, taking both the public and the private sectors, it is perhaps fair to say that the art and science of Corporate Planning has still not come up to the required level. While State planning at the national level has advanced considerably, there is a serious shortfull in the standard of planning if we look at the level of individual organisations, whether in Government or Industry, both in public and in private sectors. There could be good reasons for this such as absence of adequate data, uncertainity of the development process itself, vagaries of Government policy, distortions of a protected market etc. But it is these very weaknesses that should make the enterprises more aware of the need to undertake planning more seriously and more realistically than has been done in the past.

It will not be much of an exaggeration if it is said that even now much of our planning is done from the top to the bottom, *i.e.*, from the national level to the field level rather than from the micro corporate level to the macro economy level. This is an unsatisfactory situation and could be a serious factor undermining the effectiveness of the organisation. Unless plans are built up from the bottom, they can create difficulties in communication which, in turn, jeopardise their implementation and ultimate success. Planning to the effective has therefore to be both from bottom upwards as well as top downwards as it is ideally a two-way process.

There are some other aspects of organisational practice which could help mutual understanding within the organisation. Consider the need for demarcating the respective roles of the individual as well as of the organisations. The absence of a clear demarcation of responsibilities often leads to poor performance and accountability. Here again, there is so much that could be done to improve understanding of the organisation and the role of the individual in the organisation and there by contribute more to the effective organisational and managerial functioning.

Another area which requires urgent attention for improving managerial effectiveness through communication is performance evaluation. We talk of objectivity in performance evaluation but seem to have done precious little by way of achieving this. Nothing is more inimical to the motivation and effectiveness of individuals and organisations than unsatisfactory appraisal of performance. Very often, the motivation for good performance becomes the first casualty in setting up a peformance evaluation system. And this is caused by avoidable gaps in communication. Unless the performance of individual managers is assessed against pre-determined targets, the evaluation is bound to have a high degree of subjectivity in it. The targets of performance should also not be set unilaterally by either the assessor or the assessee. It has to be a mutually agreed target if it is to be understood properly for enabling the manager to strive to reach it. Along with corporate planning, I would therefore say that greater use of mutually agreed target setting for evaluation of performance would go a long way in communicating the requirements of the organisation vis-a-vis the manager and thereby improve his effectiveness. Quantification of targets could be a great help in this effort. It is my submission that organisations should give more attention to the estimation of performance standards in quantifiable terms. There is much greater scope for this than what has so far been perceived. Even in staff responsibilities, quantitative goal-setting is both feasible and possible.

There is a great deal of literature which has been developed on the merits of participative management for improving organisational effectiveness. The Government have recognised this and it was included as an important part of the Government's new economic programme. The scope for improving organisational productivity through participative management is tremendous. We have not even been able to touch the tip of the potential of this technique. Basically, participation can take place only through better communication. Better communication will lead to greater participation. Hence, participative approach in managerial decision-making can considerably help in the improvement of communication and efficiency of the organisation. This needs to be attempted at all levels I— the public enterprises it has been accepted that the effort should be to encourage participation at the shop-floor, at the plant level and wherever possible even on the Board of Directors. The difficulty exprienced in implementing the scheme has itself many lessons. One of the important reasons seems to have been the inadequate appreciation and sometimes unfounded doubt both on the part of the management as well as on the part of the employees regarding the benefit that could be drived from this. This is a case where an instrument to improve communication has itself become a victim of mis-understanding and mis-communication.

There is a need also to stress on the capability to receive and understand a message. Empathetic listening in order to understand what is happening within the organisation is of utmost importance. It is not enough for managers to communicate what they have to say. It is important not only to listen but also to try and understand the information, the feeling, the aspirations even the frustrations of other. Our concern should be with the entire atmosphere of the organisation which governs relationships. Mutual trust and understanding can build only on such empathy. This is the sure way of achieving greater understading, conesion, a sense of purpose and commitment in any organisation, which are so necessary to achieve better managerial effectiveness.

The subject of communication for managerial effectiveness thus covers many aspects of management. Communication is the central and critical chord which can bind the people working in the organisation together in the pursuit of common and well understood goals. The need for integrating corporate objectives with those of the individual managers is an important plank of this policy. Planning, excution of plans, evaluation of performance, participation in managerial decision-making are some of the essential features of communication, for achieving better levels of managerial performance through improved communication. Improving communication needs understanding of the environment, the organisation and above all the employees. The pursuit of such a total concept of communication will need much great imagination and innovation on the part of the managements in the coming years.

The software of communication includes management of inter-personal communication, intra-personal foundation for inter-personal communication, group communication and performance, and managing organisational communication. The software of communication is extremely important and needs emphasis and reiteration. In today's world, however, no analysis on communication for managerial effectiveness would be complete without a pointed mention of the hardware aspect of communication, which is also popularly known as the communication technology—for better or for worse. The use of mathematics as a language was perhaps the starting point of this new communication process before the Computers arrived. The role of this communication technology in the post-industrial society where mode of production is no longer mere extractive (pre-industrial society) or fabrication (industrial society) but one of processing and recycling services—is tremedous in transforming the resources, in changing time perspective and even in giving a new direction to technology. The process is so fast that it is difficult even to grasp. This hardware not only makes communication easier to work with a full range of copiers; duplicators, computer printers and video recorders which not only reproduce but can reduce, collate or even print, if necessary, but also make communication accessible across continental boundaries through video conferencing. Tele-copier, trans-receivrers, communicating typewriters that transmit information accross town or across country in minutes have already arrived in the world of today, not forgetting the electronic data-cum processing which could enable us to type, store, revise and retrieve communication data in a lot less time giving a lot more time to create and perfect it.

To sum up, it is necessary to recognise the tool of communication as one of the most powerful ingredients of effective managerial leadership. Many organisations have rich and deeply textured agenda, impressive plans and objectives of action and a vision of their future strategy. Without communication nothing gets realised. A leader can enthuse his colleagues and his organisation through communication. He also empowers others through communication in a participative management mode. A leader can chose from the available software and hardware communication technology to be used in the organisation for the organisation and by the organisation. Mastery of communication is inseparable from effective leadership. In my own personal experience, I have seen the tremendous power and usefulness of this tool. The effectiveness of the Bureau of Public Enterprises, as a catalytic agent for India's public sector, can be measured by the impact it made in communicating the goals and aspirations shared by all the public enterprises in the country. The response to the clarion calls given by the Bureau of Public Enterprises to all the public enterprises in the country to improve productivity and to improve project management through national level conferences held in 1981 and 1982 was a direct evidence of this. When the "performance aims and financial targets" of public enterprises in the Department of Mines and Department of Steel, were articulated in 1983 and 1984 as "agreed" benchmarks of improved production and profitability for the public enterprises in these two Departments, the enthusiasm that was galvanised was the single most important factor in bringing about a managerial turnaround in several of these enterprises. It also ushered in a new organisational culture whereby the enterprises effectively evaluated their own performance against their targets and shared the results of their own evaluation with Government. A leader can use communication effectively to penetrate the barriers of organisational bureaucracy. It is not a coincidence that excellent organisations around the world display this ability of using communication—

whether it is through their own rich ways of communicating informally or through other special and ad-hoc devices—to bring about a measure of organisational fluidity. It is also not a coincidence that these excellent organisations stand in sharp contrast to the whole lot of other organisations where the Managers hardly meet and talk to each other, where the Production Managers and Maintenance Engineers operate at cross purposes, where the R and D Managers and the Product Development Managers do not share their thoughts freely, where the collegues miss the excitement of peer versus peer communication in competitive situations and can never break the barrier of formal communication and organisational bureaucracy. The intensity of communication with an insistance on informality using first names from the Chairman to the lowest rung of the employee ladder, an entirely open system of seating in offices with desks of different seniority and status intermingled with desks of Departmental Managers, Directors and even the Chief Executives (some American and European Companies today advocate installation of escalators rather than elevators to ensure visibility of colleagues in the organisation) and generally an "open door" policy can add up to a virtual new ambience of communication—of keeping in constant informal contact. The new concepts of Management by Walking About or Management By Wandering Around are not any less significant. What all this adds up to is lots and lotes of communication. Communication is not mere articulation. Effective communication can even be achieved by wordlessness. Mutual trust and confidence, empathy, "shared values" in an organisation are the various languages of effective communication The message is to keep in touch, to communicate, to share one's glories and one's defeats, to share one's concerns and anexieties. Communication should create meaning. Communication should create understanding. Today, the name of the successful game is communication. The name of the game is leadership through communication and effectiveness through communication and corporate cohesiveness through communication.

2

Lifeline to the Global Network

While the technology pundits have been predicting that the day when electronic media will displace paper for all company communications is not far off, paper refuses to be banished from the world of business. Both internally and outside organisations, paper remains an important medium for communications. Paper has well proven advantages.

Paper-based information is instantly comprehensible. You do not need special equipment to extract or interpret its content. By the same token, its permanent, tangible from means that you can carry it around with you, show it to other people and, not least of all considerations, rely on its immediate acceptability as a legal document. Paper is an aesthetically appealing medium, too. You can dress up your message with different type faces, graphics and illustrations. But paper also has some considerable drawbacks.

As a medium for communicating information, it is slow and cumbersome. Postal services do not have the degree of reliability which business often requires. Paper is expensive to handle and costly to store. It also presents retrieval problems because of the inflexibility of filing systems and the fallibility of those who file papers. There is no doubt that paper is being strongly challenged by the newer forms of electronic media which transcend these kinds of limitations and offer some unique advantages of their own for certain communications purposes. Electronic systems also represent an alternative to that other mainstay, or bane, of the manager's life, the telephone.

While the telephone which sits on every desk offers the theoretical possibility of instant personal communications, about 80 per cent of calls dialled fail to make the right connections. The call is misdialled or misrouted, but more often that not, people are either not at their desks, in a meeting or the line is engaged. If a call is successfully connected, there is a high chance that it is an inconvenient time from the recipient's point of view.

When ICL carried out market research for their telephone-cum-computer terminal, the One Per Desk, unscheduled interruptions largely because of phone calls came out as the most irritating feature of the manager's working day. It is a finding which is echoed by other research. So in their respective ways, traditional forms of communication have distinct drawbacks. The newer forms of electronic communications represent an advance in certain important respects.

Electronic Mail

After word processing, the office technology which attracts most interest is probably electronic mail. It is, after all, a natural step from the preparation of text on a computer-based system to consider its transmission electronically. It offers the advantage of capitalising on the speed of the system: there are no intervening handling stages to slow the process down, as with paper-based text communications. In most cases, it is a question of pushing a few buttons, and the message or document reaches its destination almost instantaneously.

Public electronic mail services, such as Telecom Gold, and internal company systems operate on the same principles. A central computer hold the subscribers' 'mailboxes', protions of computer memory, to which messages are addressed and which only subscribers can open with the aid of their passwurds. On any of the public services, access to the electronic mail system will be possible from any suitable terminal connected by a modern over the public telephone network. Most will accept a wide range of terminals including suitably equipped electronic typewriters, desk-top computers and, most importantly from the travelling executive's or salesman's point of view, one of the many briefcase or transportable computers. As the trend continues, more micros incorporate modems and communications software as part of the package. Even where they do not, the hardware and software cost of adding communications to a micro starts at around £200.

The mailbox concept means that communications are not limited by place-to-place constraints. Regardless of where a subscriber may be, a telephone is all that is needed to provide someone with access to the service.

Exactly the same principles apply to a company electronic mail system, the main difference being that the mailbox facilities will be provided by the organisation's own computer.

Electronic mail is an asynchronous form of communication, like the mail, where transmission and receipt of messages are separated in time, but with the difference that the whole process is dramatically compressed. This gives electronic mail some unique characteristics that make it faster than the post and more dependable than hit-and-miss telephone calls. Unlike telephone calls, the message always gets through, and unlike the postal system, the message is delivered in microseconds.

When Telecom Gold researched the potential for electronic mail, it discovered that a significant proportion of business calls are requests for further information. In other words' the complete answer could not be provided there and then and depended on searching files or other sources. In these circumstances, electronic mail provides a practical alternative to the telephone. A caller asks for information which is returned by the recipient as and when it is available. Again, there is no problem of getting the message through; as soon as it is sent, it can be read. Provided that users on the system follow the discipline of looking at their mailboxes two or three times a day wherever they might be, most querries can be answered within twenty-four hours Telecom Gold provides a paging backup for subscribers who want to know as soon as a messages arrives in their mailboxes. But regular users will scan their mail frequently as a matter of habit. When the time wasted in telephone tag is taken into account, the typical delay between sending a messages and waiting for a reply with electronic mail represent a considerable improvement. This is only one way of looking at what it has to offer. Users who have thought through the unique possibilities of electronic mail, rather than considering it as a straights forward alternative to the telephone or the mail are generally those who have made the most of the medium.

It obviously appeals to those who are working out of office hours who need to let others know about decisions or new developments. With electronic mail, the message can be sent through without delay. Nor is it limited to one-to-one communications. In no more time than it takes to send a message to one person's mailbox, electronic mail can transmit copies to as many additional destinations as the sender requires. Thus, a company which wants to keep its travelling salesforce informed of stock and price changes, can issue an up-date bulletin which will be in the salesmen's mailboxes as soon as it is sent.

As things stand at present, the business user has the choice of half a dozen or so public electronic mail services. While they share several basic features, they differ at the time of writing in various ways. Some, like Istel's Comet service, cover the UK only. Geisco's Quick-Com is international in scope. Telecom Gold provides coverage in certain overseas countries.

Aside from their basic electronic mailbox facilities, services enable subscribers to send and receive telexes through their mailboxes a facility which significantly extends the reach of electronic mail. Some subscribers, according to Telecom Gold, initially come on to the service to take advantage of the telex dimension and only look at electronic mail later. The advantage of getting on to telex in this way is that no dedicated equipment is needed and telexes can be sent and collected with the same freedom as other electronic mail.

There are other service refinements. Where a company wishes to communicate regularly with salesmen, other branches and customers or suppliers, it can set up its own database of information on Telecom Gold and create what is in effect a closed uses group. To all intents and purposes, this amounts to a private network run and managed by Telecom Gold.

When it comes to costs, there is no simple means of comparison between the various electronic mail services. Each charges its subscribers according to different criteria. The various charge elements can include registration, connect time (divided into peak and off-peak rates), computer time, length of messages, the multiple address of individual messages, storage charges for the number of messages left on the system, telex transmission and receipt, a minimum monthly charge and so on. Only one company, Istel, charges for its service on a fixed monthly basis for a mailbox regardless of use. This becomes increasingly attractive the more use the subscriber makes of the service. Many small companies, by contrast, could be irregular users. Telecom Gold has introduced a special tariff structure in recognition of the needs of the less-intensive user. An exhaustive account of the comparative costs involved in communicating using the post, telex, teletex and electronic mail is given by the National Computing Centre's publication Cost-effective Message Transmission by Robyn Bray (John Wiley £5.95). It shows clearly why there is no simple answer to what is a quite reasonable question since there are so many variables in the services' charging structures. Frequency of use, local or long-distance transmission, length of message are some of the factors which can drastically alter the answer. What can be said is that electronic mail can be a cost-effeciive means of communication for businesses. As with all forms of technology, the real answer lies not simply in the comparison between the cost of sending a message through the post or using eletronic mail but in a trade-off between these and the benefits and advantages which the respective services offer. It also calls for an evaluation of the penalties of using less reliable forms of communication.

One of the obvious problems with electronic mail services as they as currently operated is that they are competitive and competitive and non-communicating. This need not initially be a problem if a company goes on to a service for its own internal use, or to connect up with a small community of suppliers and customers. But as usage grows, and more people become subscribers, there is bound to be inconvenience as would-be communicators discover that they are on different services. It is likely, though, that one service will emerge as the front runner in the next few years. It is also possible that some kind of inter-change will be possible between different services. But there is no immediate prospect of this happening.

Electronic mail users of all the services put together can still only be counted in scores of thousands, a fraction of the telex population. But electronic mail has been forecast to rival the telephone in business popularity during the 1990s. By then, the whole process should have become far easier.

Currently, one practical aspect of usage which can be a substantial disincentive to users is the burden that logging-on to the service may represent. There may be thirty alphanumeric characters to be punched to negotiate the various passwords and codes to access a service. The position can become almost nightmarishly confusing when, as is quite likely, a user wants to subscribe to electronic mail and other on-line information services, each with their log-on procedures, codes and pass-words. Fortunately, there is a handy remedy.

There are modems, along with their attendant computer software, which allow the user to automate the whole process. Auto-dial modems will call the relevant telephone number and then negotiate the various passwords and procedures to get the subscriber on to the service. This can save a considerable amount of keyboard-bashing and potential frustration. If your finger slips and you press the wrong key, or you simply cannot remember all the necessary codes, you must start again. Most services lock you out after three unsuccessful attempts in the interests of seeurity on the assumption that pass-word jugglers might be illegal tamperers with the system.

As with most electronic systems, the dividing line between one service or another is often blurred. Electronic mail is no exception and has some features in common with viewdata which, although not primarily intended as a messaging system, provide a mailbox-type facility for system users.

Viewdata

Developed originally in the U.K. viewdata is a simplified mean of accessing and displaying information held on computer. Viewdata was designed to run on specially adapted television sets using the public telephone network as the communications system. This was the basis for Prestel, the world's first public viewdata service. When the Post Office launched Prestel in 1981, it believed that it was laying the foundations for a national electronic information service which would appeal primarily ~~to~~ the domestic market.

Viewdata systems go a long way to make life easy of the user. Unlike the average computer database. viewdata organises organises information in pages, a page being equivalent to a screenful of information. To take it simple to find your way round, the viewdata database is organised on a branching, tree-like structure. You can switch on and go straight to a particular page. But if you do not know exactly where you want to go, you begin with a main menu which branches into a number of sub-menus and so on until and reach the information you are searching for, remain, unlike the average computer system, viewdata a uses clearer, larger characters and employs labeur and graphics to brighten the presentation of data. In Prestel's case, the graphics have a jagged, like appearance. In time, graphics will become another and more naturalistic in appearance. something which is already possible with some viewdata technologies. The aim of viewdata is to take computer-based information readily accessible to the layman.

Originally, Prestel set out to provide information everything from the stars (the astrological variety recipes to train timetables, cinema programmes weather forecasts. But events have shown that the market thought otherwise. When the service was reached, British Telecom talked in terms of reaching a million subscribers, mainly in the domestic market. By mid-1985, the tally was 59,000. Aside anything else, the service proved too expensive have mass-market appeal and BT underestimated appeal to business: 55 per cent of subscribers are the business sector.

Accordingly, many of the 1200 plus information considers aim their services primarily at companies, regulary up-dated information on share price, commodity, exchange rates and other financial and business data is among the attractions for business users. Prestel also operates in another mode.

Alongside its general, publicly accessible services, there is a closed user group facility, which enables an organisation to rent a slice of the service for its own private use. In effect, this is a bureau service provided on the public network. Several other privately-run bureaux provide comparable services. A number of large companies have also set up their own internal viewdata systems linking head office with branches and their field sales force.

Companies have realised the value of viewdata as a means of conveniently reaching their home-based salesforces. Just as electronic mail is a useful way of extending communications beyond conventional office hours, so information on product lines, stock holding and so on can be accessed through view-data at the end of the working day.

One of viewdata's advantages is its comparative cheapness. A viewdata terminal, keyboard and modem work out cheaper than a conventional computer terminal, although with developments in computer technology, the gap is steadily closing. Alternatively, most microcomputers can easily be adapted with the appropriate modem and software to receive viewdata. The other plus-point, and the one which represented a major concession to those who complain about the difficulty of using computers, is the simplicity of viewdata.

Initially, Prestel was a non-way system for issuing information. When it was made interactive so that subscribers could put in their own data, it opened up a fresh spectrum of opportunities. Thus, salesforces can log details of orders taken, as well as check company data. This two-way communications facility has broadened the scope for domestic services, too. Telemarketing became possible.

Club 405 was launched to test the potential for home shopping along with the supply of other services in the Midlands. Homelink, Nottingham Building Society's pioneering national home-banking and home-shopping service, has provided shops and sales organisations with the chance of expanding their display window electronically. Local butchers, gift shops and food stores have been among the retailers to experiment with home shopping. Typically, these services are tied in with mail-order, in the case of food stores. with local delivery services.

It remains to be seen just how significant home shopping, and home banking (the Royal Bank of Scotland was the first bank to offer a viewdata-based service) will become. But the critical mass has yet to be reached in the domestic market which would make telemarketing a glittering propsect for the retail business as a whole. Those who have thought things out carefully, though, have met with more success than those who have simply plunged in without considering viewdata's pros and cons. So for example, its graphics are limited and cannot compete with the high-gloss sales catalogue. Yet a London shop selling glassware successfully adapted Prestel's graphics to illustrate styles and shapes of glasses and so on.

In a business-to-business environment, though, this constraint need not be important. What companies are doing successfully is to link their major suppliers, or customers, to their computer-based stock systems, so that orders can be placed with greater speed and efficiency than they can with conventional systems. While viewdata and electronic mail are ways of escaping from the limitations of paper for exchanging information and ordering, they are not a complete answer. Sometimes there is no escape from paper.

Facsimile

When it is essential to send an exact copy of a document, or where graphics and illustrations are an integral par, of the message, paper is unavoidable. In these cases, facsimile can be used to accelerate the transmission of documents between two points. Worldwide, the installed facsimile base in 1985 was estimated to be nearly 1.5 million, rivalling the number of telex machines. Britain had about 45,000 facsimile machines installed, making it the largest user in Europe.

In recent years, facsimile, or fax, in common with other technologies, has evolved considerably. Today's transceivers produce sharper, better images and operate faster. The problem here, as in all areas of electronic communications, is standards. As with other internationally used telecommunications technologies, these have to be established on a global scale. Fax, along with other telecommunications standards, are the province of a regulatory body commonly known as the CCITT.

To date, technological evolution has resulted in three generations. or groups. of fax machines. In 1985, the CCITT announced the standard for group four fax standards. Each successive group, when introduced, represents an advance over the earlier in terms of a higher speed of operation and improved image. Group three models, based on digital technology, can transmit an A4 page in under one minute, group two takes three minutes while group one, now considered obsolete; takes six minutes.

Although they are downwardly compatible, in that the latest machines can talk to earlier groups, the reverse is not true. While the fax population is growing rapidly, this means of communications is likely to be most use to these who need to send documents back and forth regularly and are in a position to ensure compatibility. According to British Telecom International, which publishes a directory of fax users, the biggest concentrations of users are to be found in the legal and accountancy sectors (25 per cent) followed by manufacturing (10 per cent), engineering (15 per cent) and financial services (11 per cent).

Until recently, fax, like telex, was limited to communications between two fixed points. The development of portable fax machines has introduced a new geographical freedom to this mode pf communications for those who need it.

Telex and Teletext

If few businesses can confidently be expected to have fax machines, few of any size are likely to be without telex. The great attraction of the telex net-work is that it is well established, with almost one and a half million subscribers world-wide in more than 200 couutries. After the telephone, it is the most universally used form of business telecommunications. However, it is beginning to show its age.

Compared with electronic mail, it is snail-paced. Telex transmits at a rate of 50 bits per second, or 10 characters per second, compared with Telecom Gold's 1200 bps, or 150 cps. Telex also uses a limited 5-bit code which cannot even cope with lower case characters, punctuation, pound, dollar or percentage symbols. It is also point-to-point rather than person-to-person. Line failures and connection difficulties, associated with international calls, are likely to be aggravated by the yearly growth in traffic. In the longer-term, it seems destined to be phased out in favour of other services, but not in the short term. It will be kept going for some time. British Telecom announced in 1985 that it is giving its ageing service e seventy-million pound facelife.

As explained earlier in this chapter, the attraction of telex to the smaller company is greater now than at any time in the past, ironically because of the versatility of electronic mail. Up until the addition of the telex facility by electronic mail providers, it was necessary to have special telex equipment and a leased line to get on to the telex network. Now any terminal suitable for electronic mail can send and receive telexes from the mailbox.

Despite its advantages to many smaller companies, the cost of using electronic mail for telex becomes steep if the volume of traffic is high. Currently, users on some services are charged 50p per incoming telex.

One of the services which will ultimately replace telex as a poiht-to-point means of communication is teletex. This was inaugurated in the UK in 1985, but is having a slow start as an international service because of problems with standards and equipment approval.

Teletex primarily uses the existing telephone network, although there are links with telex's dedicated telegraph system, to enable word processors and other-generating devices to transmit messages through the service, Speed of transmission, at 2400 bits per second, will be 30 times faster than telex, Teletex suffers from none of telex's limiting foctors: there is a full character set and users will have all the advantages of word processing style editing. But eo far, lack of agreement on standards has slowed down its introduction and only a handful of terminals have been approved for teletex use in the UK. In the meantime, telex continues to thrive. Indeed, it is perfectly feasible that telex will coexist for many years alongside more advanced communications systems.

Telephone Systems

Athough British Telecom has embarked on the digitisation of the public telephone network, it may well not be until the turn of the century that the transformation will be complete. There will be a number of benefits for business.

At present, the telephone network is still substantially analogue in nature. This means that the signals it carries vary continuously. Digital transmission, by contrast, requires all signals to be in binary code form, the natural language of computers. The fact that the public telephone network is predominantly analogue is why it is necessary for computers to be connected by modems. These translate the computer's binary signals into pulsed tones which can travel over the network and then be comprehensible to another computer. When digitisation is complete voice, as well as data, will be transmitted in binary code. A digital network will mean faster connections and better quality-sound for voice and data communications. By this stage, every company will need a digital exchange on its premises to take advantage of the network's improved performance. In the meantime, the new generation of private branch exchanges give companies a far greater range of features for users,

With the liberalisation of telecommunications following. The Telecommunications Act 1981, there is a wider choice of exchanges on the market. Small companies, in particular, have benefited from the change in the marketing of telephone systems. All the new generation of exchanges designed to cater for companies with from two to about 30 incoming lines and up to 100 or so extensions are microprocessor based. They therefore share many of the same features available only on larger exchanges up until a few years ago.

These exchanges, many of which come in digital and analogue versions. are electronic and programmable (they are sometimes known as stored programme control exchanges or SPCs, another piece of jargon to untangle). Their features are intended to maximise the efficiency of voice communications and give business greater control of their telecommunications traffic. Modern exchanges, including the Herald, Ensign, Viceroy and Regent, which company, could include some or all of the following kinds of feature.

Abbreviated dialling enables outside numbers of be stored and dialled using a two or four digit code.

Call pick-up means that any extension can pick up another's calls which can represent a saving on exchange lines.

Direct inward dialling to an extension can give outside callers more immediate access to a particular individual or department.

Repeat last number: when a number you are trying to reach is engaged, it can be memorised by the exchange and redialled by pressing a single button.

Call logging is for those who want to achieve tighter control of their telecommunications costs. A printer plugged into a special socket in the exchange records outgoing calls by extension, duration and so on.

Enquiry calls can be made on systems which allow an incoming call to be held while another extension is rung.

Call diversion automatically reroutes a call from the the primary extension to another nominated extension.

Extension group hunting: if one extension is busy, the exchange will hunt it finds one free within a designated group of extensions.

Conference calls of between six or more people, depending on the system, are possible with most modern exchanges.

Call barring prevents certain extensions from making unauthorised calls. for example overseas, or all extensions from making such calls after a certain time.

These kinds of features can help to free the bottle-necks which are created with older style exchanges and, at the same time, help the business in a number of ways. It is not difficult, for example, to see that facilities such as direct inward dialling could improve the company's communications with the outside world by giving customers better access to service departments.

At the same time, the latest exchanges should enable companies to make the most cost-effective use of the telephone system. Since the load on telephone operators is reduced mainly to handling incoming calls, it may be possible to manage with fewer operators or to divide a single operator's time between the switchboard and other work. In common with other microelectronic equipment, the cost of exchanges has come down. In 1985, they worked out, typically, at £`00 an extension and some of the smaller exchanges cost around £200 an extension. This is about half the price of a few years ago.

While exchanges themselves have been enhanced with the aid of microprocessors, so, too, have telephones. Some of these functions, typically one-button re-dial and telephone number storage, are incorporated in feature phones. Starting at under £100 for models with limited facilities, they go up to £200 or 300. Cordless telephones, too, have something to offer the company where staff are regularly away from their desks, but still need to keep in touch.

Integration of voice and data is still some way off, but those terminals which combine telephone and computer facilities in one unit—ICL's OPD, STC's Executel, Mitel's Kontact and Northern Telecom's Display phone—hint at the way things are more. Although they represent different interpretations of what precisely a manager wants from this new form of hybrid terminal, they are intended to provide practical solutions to the pressures which undermine executive efficiency.

These telephone-cum-computers variously allow executives to create their own telephone directories of contracts which can be auto-dialled by the machine, access electronic mail and viewdata services, log-on to other computer databases, store and manipulate data. At one end of the scale, the Mitel machine is more of a full-blow micro with advanced telephone facilities, while the Displayphone is more of a sophisticated telephone with some computer terminal features. The OPD is the exception in having a limited, programmable answering machine so that callers can receive some kind of reply when the terminal is unmanned.

For many small companies, the unmanned telephone is a potential business loser. But the development of versatile telephone answering machines means that no organisation need to be without the means of taking orders or recording their callers' messages. With the remote phone-in feature provided with many models, it is possible to pick up the messages even when you are away from the office. Either as a means for maintaining 'presence' out-of hours, or during the working day, telephone answering machines have considerable value for the small business.

British Telecom has recently introduced an alternative to answering services:

> Voicebank, a form of electronic voice mail, similar in principle to the text-based system. Subscribers have a voice mailbox on a central computer which callers can dial up over the telephone system and leave verbal messages. These are stored in digital form by the computer and retrieved by the subscriber with a unique password.

Now, of course, it is also possible to keep in touch on the move with one of the paging services, such as those run by British Telecom and Air Call. With the development of more versatile receivers, including those with digital displays, it is possible to transmit brief messages rather than all-purpose bleeps. The mobile telephone is also entering a new era with the advent of cellular radio. The promises to overcome the geographical limitatiyns and reception problems of radio-telephones by achieving consistent coverage of the country with a honeycomb of 'cells', each with their own transmitters. Two competing services, Cellnet jointly owned by British Telecom and Securicor, and Racal's Vodaphone services, came onto the air in early 1985. Initially, cellular radio was available in London and other metropolitan areas but should spread rapidly: the Government requires the services to cover 90 per cent of the population by 1990.

Although the cost of cellular radio sets in 1985 was around £1500, this should, in common with the cost of most other microelectronic products, come down in due course. Soon, there need be no reason to be beyond reach of the telephone, a prospect which will gladden some, but by no means all.

These new systems are a far cry from the facilities with which business has been run up until now. But as is often the case, the technological possibilities are several steps ahead of a general understanding of the applications. More facilities do not necessarily mean better management. Executives complain of being overwhelmed with information and intrusions. There is obviously a real danger that this burgeoning range of electronic communications systems could threaten to overwhelm the businessman. Alongside the other skills which will have to be developed is the managerial ability to ensure that technology remains the servant of business and that the roles are not reversed.

Summary

Electronic mail provides a number of unique facilities which mean that it cannot simply be considered as an alternative to telephone calls on the one hand and postal services on the other.

Viewdata offers a means of giving inexperienced users access to computer-based information.

Telemarketing, using Prestel, is now practicable, but needs to be carefully thought through.

Continuing technical development of facsimile systems widens the applications for electronic means of document communication.

With the lastest developments in telecommunications, including store-and-forward voice messaging and cellular radio, companies need not be out of touch with customers and suppliers when staff are out of the office.

3

Internal Communications

It's a spartan existence on America's last frontier, where the Alyeska Pipeline Service Company is laying the trans-Alaskan pipeline, the most expensive construction project in history. They work up to twelve hours a day, seven days a week, in which temperatures can fall to 55 below freezing! There are few women—no liquor. The only contact with the outside world is by radio telephone.

But the workers are kept sweet and hard working by big money—around $2,000 a month, and by (for construction workers) lush camp conditions such as carpeted, well-furnished rooms, well-stocked libraries and daily movies.

Cash is a crude but powerful method of communicating with the workers when the job is especially tough. One reason is the symbolic significance of money. During the national mineworkers' strike in the UK in 1972 one union leader said: 'Our men spend all day in dangerous, unhealthy jobs, yet their daughters, working as secretaries, earn as much as they do.' How much pay-turmoil is really about recognition and self respect—both much harder to give than money.

Subtler Methods Needed

Workers in many factories find it difficult to feel much self-respect: 'You'd treat a dog better than this, give it a longer leash', a car worker complained. 'A man's work station is the length of the car body plus three feet either end and he has to stay in it'. In some plants a man can't even go to the lavatory until the spare man arrives to take his place on the track.

"When I'm here my mind's a blank. I make it go a black.' It takes more than incentives to cut through cynicism as deep as this. Subtler communication techniques are needed.

I've heard of bakery workers who were so turned-off with their jobs that they simply walked out in mid-shift and didn't even come back for their wages.

Walter Reuther, the American union boss, in describing the plight of many industrial workers, evoked a Chaplinesque vision of men crushed in the cogs: 'The prospect of tightening bolts every ten minutes for eight hours a day for thirty years doesn't exactly lift the human spirit.'

The facts of industrial life can cause a tremendous built-up of frustration and resentment which vents itself in poor work, absenteeism, hostility to management—even outright violence. In Working for Ford Hugh.Benyon reports bostic bombs being hurled by frustrated workers into rubbish dumps at one of Ford's UK plants.

Turned-off Workers

How many bruising confrontations in industry stem for these pent-up frustrations? At a Liverpool factory in 1975 management and workers locked horns over the vital issue of where the wages should be handed out. The workers felt so 'bolshy' that they refused to allow management into the factory to distribute them there. Management retaliated by stopping workers going into the office block and collecting them there. A compromise was worked out. The wages were handed out through a side-window while workers queued in the rain.

How can you communicate with your work force in spite of the frustrations and aggression that may exist? One hundred and thirty years ago, Disraeli wrote about 'two nations . . . as ignorant of each other's habits, thoughts and feelings as if they were dwellers in different zones or inhabitants of different planets'. Today a cleavage in social ethics still exists, and it separates the manager from his work force—unless he knows how to bridge the gap.

Close co-operation between the two sides of industry during the three-day week period in 1974 shows that genuine communication can take plaee. But too many managers still regard industrial relations as somebody else's business. Hugh Parker, head of McKinsey's consultancy operation in the UK points out that 'people who manage don't identify themselves with the interests of the managed. They stay aloof—at arm's length from the workers'. Here are some techniques for getting closer to your work force.

Group Sessions

Many companies, such as the Japanese giant, Matsushita, find that the group session attended once a week, say, by the entire staff of a section or department of division is an effective communication method.

The meetings should be as informal as possible so that everyone is encouraged to talk. In a relaxed atmosphere management can explain its plans and policies and tell the employees wnat is happening to the goods they are producing—remind them of their important contribution.

Work can be freely discussed. improvements suggested, and the workers can buttonhole their bosses and air their grievances. Policies can be explained. The advantage of doing it this way is that once the whole group accepts the need for a change of plan or procedure, individuals who are hostile to management tend to adjust to the new conformity. Some men take pride in defying management but think twice before opposing their own work mates.

Informal Meetings with Workers' Representatives

An engineering firm's management which in previous years had met union officials only at times of crisis decided to ask the union to meet them regularly, reason or no reason. So, once a week the two sides met—just sat and talked informally. For the first time each side found itself really listening and being interested in the other. Each side was able to explain its own point of view and, because of the informal atmosphere, really wanted to learn the other side's view.

Each meeting brought a quick exchange of process that brought both sides closer to their common objective—compromise, and therefore stability across the industrial board.

When the number of disputes in the factory dropped, management linked the trend with these informal meetings. Thus they soon paid for themselves many times over.

When people from the two sides of industry sit informally round the same table they begin to understand one another's viewpoint. When they sit round the table long enough and often enough they even begin to share the same values and talk the same language.

Of course the communication barriers will remain unless the unions feel that management are really listening during these meetings and will take action as a result of what they hear.

More Contact with Union Leaders

Many unions are better at fighting management than at co-operating with it to achieve joint goals. One clue in dealing with awkward union branches comes from F. M. Thrasher's book Gang based on his work with delinquent teenage gangs. He found that the best way to influence these gangs was through their leaders. By concentrating attention on the leader and showing him ways of achieving status and security—the main motives for gang membership—by other means than the gang, Thrasher was able to change the attitude of the whole gang. The rest followed the leader's example.

Perhaps, after all, the best way to deal with the militant shop steward or wildcat leader is not to isolate him, not to seek less contract but to seek more contact with him. onto the works committees. Give him special responsibilities—and therefore status. Ask him to chair staff meetings or group sessions. In this way you will involve the man and his followers in management processes.

Or carry involvement a stage further. Ask the local union branch to advise management about discipline and conditions of work—the length and times of tea-breaks, holiday and overtime arrangements and so on. This kind of direct involvement management creates a greater sense of responsibility in union members, a greater awareness of management problems.

Supervisory Interviews

Supervisory interviews, held about twice a year, can raise morale and improve communication between employee and first-line management. Supervisors who are trained to conduct these interviews should be fully briefed about aims and techniques to ensure (a very difficult task) that employees will feel free to talk without inhibition.

During the interview, the employee is given an appraisal of his performance over the past half-year together with advice about how to improve. We need to remember that many workers lose heart because they genuinely don't know how they are measuring up to company expectations: nobody ever tells them.

Then it is the employee's turn to talk about his or her problems and grievances, or about anything else they want to get off their chests.

Western Electric has found that supervisors who are involved in these interviews become less dogmatic in their ideas, more willing to take account of the feelings of their subordinates. The first-line manager is brought into closer contact with his people, perhaps in spite of himself.

Success depends largely on the social skills of the interviewer, his ability to establish an easy relationship with the other person. Thus the provision of effective company training in this field is essential. Chances of success are improved when:

(a) the scpervisor holds the interview on neutral ground and not in his own office;

(b) is careful not to show too much authority;

(c) encourages the employee (by using appropriate counselling techniques) to speak his mind;

(d) does not argue, disagree, express shock or disapproval.

The Value of Technique

Areas like there show clearly that communication is above all a technique when applied to industry.

The inevitable social and environment stresses which crop up in the industrial organization do not admit social contact between individual managers and employees in an entirely normal way. For the factory or the office is always an artificial environment in which individuals cannot choose each other's company.

The problem is compounded because of the frustration and resentments that build up in the work force as a result of tedium and discipline. Such feelings are not dissolved by cash incentives, unless they are abnormally high.

In large organizations, formal patterns of communication will always predominate. But the trick is to promote better relations by encouraging informal communication between managers and employees.

This is not something that can happen overnight with some magic gesture. It will be the product only of a consistant management policy that sets out to win and deserve the confidence of the work force. To achieve that, management must not only accept the principle of good communication, but get down to the planning of a detailed campaign.

Such a campagin might be spearheaded by the techniques describe above. But in any case, it will require the co-operation of the other side as a starting point.

Points for Discussion

Discuss 'the symbolic significance of money'.

Do you feel a cleavage exists to-day between the manager and his work force?

What is the principal value of group sessions?

What are the likely advantages to a manager in having more contact with trade union leaders?

Discuss the supervisory interview.

Meetings

No business or industrial organization can get-along without a large number of meetings (unfortunately!). Meetings, when properly run are probably the most valuable of a company's means of communication. They are certainly necessary if we are to promote:

(a) Understanding and willing acceptance of the company's policies and procedures;

(b) A correct understanding and tolerance of people's needs and desires; 'two-way' exchange of constructive suggestions and ideas; intelligent co-operation;

(c) Savings of time, of repetition and paperwork.

But meetings cost money, We have to calculate the salaries of those present, the cost of time taken by those who helped prepare for the meeting and produced the necessary documentation and the cost of lighting, heating, ventilating and perhaps even renting the meeting room. It is imperative, therefore, that we use the time spent in meetings profitably, and that the leader and participants achieve the objectives of every meetings arranged.

Meetings vary between these two extremes:

1. Highly formal, complete with chairman, secretary, agenda, usual minutes and formal rules of procedure;
2. Very informal—ad hoc meetings about current business often attended by close colleagues on first-name terms.

In the day-to-day working of an organization the first type of meeting is fairly rare. Besides this, there are many good books on formal meetings, whether they be for companies, Local Government of voluntary organizations. And as this book communicating anyway, we will content ourselves with looking at the conduct of an informal meeting.

Purposes

I have attended (and conducted on occasion!) meetings that have ended more from sheer exhaustion than for any other reason. I have attended (and still do!) meetings which I regard as a waste of time. The reason often starts with, as indeed in most forms of bad communication, an unclear and inadequate preparation. When you are thinking of calling a meeting the following rules will be helpful:

1. Establish a valid purpose for calling the meeting. A meeting may be called: (a) to give information; (b) to get information; (c) to solve a problem; or (d) to secure certain positive attitudes. The leader and participants must know at any point in the conduct of the meeting which of these four objectives is applicable.
2. Consider carefully whether the purpose could not better be achieved by some other means, such as a memorandum or a series of telephone calls.
3. Consider when the meeting should be held. Make sure all the relevant people are available, the facts of documents are to hand and that the meeting is not being held after the decision to be taken thereat should have been taken.
4. Establish who should attend. If a decision has to be reached you need people to be present who have the power to make that decision. Sometimes full participation will not be expected, as will be the case when you are calling a meeting to hear a statement of policy, a definition of responsibilities or to receive instructions.

If at all possible you will avoid inviting the 'difficult' member. He is one who talks too much or at length, constantly talks off the subject and is generally quite illogical. He is also impatient and wants a decision without a thorough investigation. He's always unwilling to consider alternatives or compromise, and makes dogmatic unsupported statements; he gives no reasons, and the points he makes always need clarification or illustration. He does not pay attention but always whispers and interrupts. And he always comes to the meeting you are conducting! He needs firm leadership, and the use of questions addressed to him will usually go a long way to disciplining him.

Unsuccessful Meetings

Before we go on to the conduct of meetings let's look briefly at the problems which occur all too often. First of all, meetings are often held for the wrong reasons, *e.g.*, the organizational structure may not have kept pace with changing needs. *Ad hoc* committees set up to deal with a particular problem sometimes become fixed. Some groups may even be meeting purely out of habit—there may be a regular Thursday morning meeting at 10.00 a.m. with nobody examining whether or not the meeting should still be taking place. There may be inadequate advance information, or faulty composition of the group. The leader may be vague about the subject or purpose There may be no provisional plan, there may be bad handling of the time factor or physical conditions may be inadequate. Meetings may be held simply because managers feel inadequate. They do not have the course to make the decisions necessary so they call a meeting; or indeed they may even use the meeting to delay making the required decision.

Meetings may also be unsuccessful because some items had apparently been decided beforehand. Or there may be too much emotion present, while lack of control may allow too many people to talk at the same time. There's always a serious problem if the chairman or leader is biased. Key issues may not be defined nor main issues clarified, so that there will be several red herrings present throoghout. Some people may never open their mouths throughout, while others may have no idea at the end of the meeting of what has been decided. Diffident members may even be discouraged or snubbed.

Then at the end the progress may not be summarized, minority views ignored and inaccurate quotation of contributions. Unsettled points may be left 'in the air', and finally the required action may not be formulated.

Correct Approach to Running a Meeting

First of all see that none of the above problems occur! Then let's think first about physical conditions. Make sure the temperature of the room is couducive to work—not too cold nor too hot. Ventilation is very important and fresh air keeps participants alert. Noise can be very distracting. There should be a bright atmosphere about the room, with comfortable furnishings—these have a definite psychological effect. Refreshments can revive people, particularly at a long meeting, but do make sure that they are not brought in during a closely argued discussion. Arrange the seating so that all members can see each other easily—an oval shaped table for larger groups can be suitable and a horsesnoe or 'U' table for groups of fourteen or over. If possible, a company should have a few properly equipped conference rooms available on the premises of different sizes and suitably sound proofed. Of course, meetings do not always have to take place in a room—a few colleagues talking in a corridor may be all that's necessary, and if the right decision is reached in those (or any) circumstances you can be assured the meeting has been successful.

There are really three stages to any meeting—before, during and after.

Before the Meeting

You have to decide what you want to achieve through the group of people who will be present. Are you out to sell them some idea, a new company policy, to solve a problem or to secure certain positive attitudes? Do you want them to take a decision that you know they will be committed to without any pressure from you.

Then you have to know the subject being discussed inside out. Do plenty of homework; collect, sort, and arrange all the relevant information. Prepare a workable timetable for your own use, apportioning relative times to major and minor issues. Be well armed in relation to possible questions and/or objections.

Prepare an agenda which is merely a list of items to be discussed; it covers all relevant points in the right order. The early items should not be controversial and important items should not be left until the very last, at which time some may have had to leave (to attend another meeting possibly!), while those remaining will naturally be tired. It assists pertinent discussion of items on the agenda if they are all divided into sub-sections if appropriate, and all items should be specific and concrete. Often for small meetings held on a regular basis agendas may be dispensed with, but even so, the leader of the meeting should always have one for his own use. Try to have the agenda sent out in good time (obviously statutory meetings have set amounts of notice which must be given), so that all members can themselves be fully informed on the issues to be discussed. If you do send a note with the agenda make sure it tells those attending what the subject is all about and that you are inviting their participation.

Adequate preparation, as in any form of communicating, will greatly help the effectiveness of the meeting, bearing in mind that all of us have opinions, prejudices and attitudes to everything under the sun. And don't forget to have any visual aids or reports ready in plenty of time.

Conducing the Meeting

Start on time. Repeat—start on time! Welcome members, especially newcomers. Emphasize the work to be done. State the topic, problem or difficulty with which the meeting is to deal. You may wish to outline the situation giving rise to the topic, and outline what is appropriate for discussion and what it not. Outline the procedure to be followed in the case of groups not meeting on a regular basis.

Define technical terms being used, and remember the subject for discussion must be simply and clearly expressed and all ambiguous words must be clarified. The vague statement of a subject is probably the cause of most futile discussion. It is often a good idea to put the subject before the meeting in the form of an impartial question; one advantage of this is that a question at least provides the framework for the answer.

People called to a meeting tend to bring their immediate problems with them. They may even have decided views on the matters they know are going to be discussed. So you must put them at case and focus their minds on the purpose of the meeting. An informal call to order is usually all that is necessary to get their attention, and then you begin your brief introduction. After this you may ask a direct question or a question of the group as a whole. The leader must draw out all relevant information, viewpoints and experiences. He or she must make sure that all available information is before the meeting and get further information from members as is necessary. He must stimulate thinking and get the meeting to examine the experience and judgement of all. The member who insists on talking must be interrupted—you can thank him for his seven points and tell him before he continues with the other seven you would like to discuss the ones just made. Everyone—both sides—at a meeting can and should be heard—but not indefinitely. Encourage those who tend to be quiet. Link the speakers together and provide the channel through which they speak. But talk yourself only when you must. Cajole the members into brevity, but try not to choke off discussion until it comes to an end. Wait until you get from the feeling of the meeting that time has come for the particular debate or argument to be would up. You, as a chairman or leader, are running the meeting, but don't make it too obvious. The top leaders keep the show going and ensure that everyone stays contented and awake, and the finest chairmen are those who use good humour, quiet tact and gentle persuasion.

Summarize the developments of the discussion from time to time and refer to any changes of opinion. State points of agreement and disagreement, state intermediate conclusions as they are reached and make sure of members' understanding and acceptance of summaries. A particularly good time to give a summary is when you notice that uniform thinking has been reached on one phase of the subject and no really new contribution is coming forward. There should, of course, be a summary when each intermediate conclusion is reached. Summaries are also useful to bring discussion back to the point and purpose of the meeting when the subject has been extended beyond profitable limits.

Establish the final conclusion reached, state the main points contributed at the meeting, mention any minor disagreements, make sure your summary is fair and that all the members understand it. It should make clear to people just what they have achieved and what further action they have committed themselves or the organization to taking.

Try to finish the meeting on time. If this looks like being impossible then ask the members if they wish to extend the meeting for another half-hour or so.

At the very end thank the members for their contribution to the group achievement.

After the Meeting

The majority of informal meetings are supposed to lead to changes in the work situation. You may wish to send a brief summary in writing to all those present, outlining the decision reached and the action to be taken as a result. In any event there should be a permanent record of what took place. If your summary at the meeting itself has been clear you won't have people saying 'Oh I didn't think we agreed to that'. People do not contest what they have created. Formal minutes and informal notes also serve as a starting point in any further meetings on similar subjects.

Committees

A committee is a person or group of persons to whom something is 'committed'. It is therefore possible for one person to form a committee—probably the most effective committee of all! It is usually a small body of people appointed by a parent body to meet to discuss particular matters which are defined in its terms of reference. Recommendations are expected to be made to the parent body, where the committee is an advisory one. But decisions are expected from a policy committee. Committees may be homogeneous where all the members are of similar interests and status, they may be mixed, or joint. Many companies have joint consultative committees (also called works councils), comprising representatives of both workers and management and meeting at weekly or monthly intervals. Normally these joint consultative committees do not negotiate conditions of work; they discuss matters of common interest to management and labour such as methods of improving efficiency, safety and welfare. The balance of management and worker participation varies, but it is usual to have equal representation or a slight bias in favour of the workers. These committees are of special value in improving communications within a company.

Most professional institutions, learned societies and voluntary organizations make extensive use of committees. The council would be the main body. There would also be a small executive committee through which most of the business is conducted, and reports thereof would be periodically presented to the council for approval.

There are several advantages of the committee system of management.

1. Committee work can be said to be a highly significant feature of modern industrial life and a sign of democratic control in that it is constituted by the free votes of an elected assembly;
2. the specialized knowledge of diverse people is pooled for the common good;
3. the continuity of the committee is assured regardless of changes in its personnel.

In addition to the joint committee mentioned above there are also standing committees, *ad hoc* or special committees, and the old favourite, sub-committees.

Standing committees, are those formed for specified purposes only. These are used mostly by local government and for Parliamentary affairs. Country councils, for example, often have a finance committee, a planning committee, a general purposes committee, etc.

Ad hoc or special committees are those formed for special investigations and are usually dissolved when their reports are submitted. The inauguration of a pension scheme or the installation of a computer are items that would be dealt with by an *ad hoc* committee whose members would have special knowledge and experience in these fields. The formation of these committees leaves the parent body free to concern itself with the major business of the institution and with policy.

Sub-committees are occasionally formed to relieve a larger committee of detailed work and their activities are limited to that particular work. Examples are a transfer committee of a board of directors or a finance committee of a governing council.

As well as a good means of communication there are intricate psychological and social motives underlying committee work. Executive control by individual to individual is sometimes fraught with complicated emotions and some inhibitions. But sitting down with others rouud a table in committee provides an opportunity to shed those inhibitions. People are there to voice opinions, exchange ideas and contribute to the decision and there is therefore a kind of anonymity which pervades committee work.

Committees generally tend to be reasonably formal, with their own rules as to quorums, proposals, resolutions, minutes and all matters of election and procedures. They make a very large and valuable contribution to industrial, local governmental and professional life of the United Kingdom and embody a proud tradition of service.

Discussion Groups

In our society more and more of the daily operations of business, education and government are being directed by groups of people—committees, boards, councils, and conferences. Certainly any business or professional man spends much of his time participating in discussions; in fact, his effectiveness in his job may be very largely determined by his skill in discussion. Although discussion varies in method from group to group, the following should serve as a good working definition: discussion is a co-operative process by which a group of persons exchange and evaluate ideas and information abont a mutual problem in order to understand or solve that problem.

There are generally two purposes of a discussion group which may be indepedent or inter-related:

(a) to exchange ideas or opinions; and
(b) to reach an agreement or make a decision.

The least any discussion can do is to inform each participant of other members' knowledge and opinions about the subject under consideration. Sometimes this is the only purpose of the discussion but often the exchange of ideas is merely a preliminary to making a decision. In either case the pooling of information and the expression of the divergent opinion are very valuable methods of getting a broad understanding of the problem and of providing a sound basis for making a decision. If it is desired to reach an agreement there is no doubt that through the give and take of discussion individual beliefs are often modified and a consensus reached. If a consensus should prove impossible at least the range of disagreement may be sufficiently narrowed so that a clear understanding of the remaining basic differences are arrived at.

The various types of discussion group with which you and I may be expected to be involved are: Study groups, Committee Meetings, Panel discussions, or Symposium discussions.

A study group is normally quite an informal affair. A speech or lecture is given, after which there is a mutual exchange of information. The ideas and information exchanged means that those present learn something from each other as in the case of conventions or seminars where men and women in the same business profession tell each other of experiences they have had or detail the results of their research or method of dealing with common problems.

We have already dealt with Committee Meetings.

Panel Discussions

Where a group is too large to engage in effective discussion or many of its members are too uninformed for such a discussion be mutually profitable, a small group—usually about three to six individuals—often discusses the problem on a platform before a larger group. The individuals in the panel are chosen because they are well informed on the particular topic and can supply the facts needed for intelligent discussion or because all of them are known to represent points of view held by a considerable part of the audience and can act as spokesmen to express these viewpoints.

The Symposium Discussion

Very common in America. They arise where a small group of people usually four or five ~~give~~ a series of short six or seven minute speeches each presenting a different viewpoint or aspect of the particular subject being discussed. They are common at large conventions were experts are asked to talk on varying subjects or several aspects of the same topic and they are also used to report the findings of various groups attending a conference.

Both the symposium and panel discussion are often followed by an open forum, where the participants answer questions put by those in the audience. The general principle of the symposium and panel discussion is that one small group do most of the talking while the larger group listens and asks questions.

When leading a discussion, state the topic, problem or difficulty with which the meeting is to deal, outline the situation giving rise to the topic problem or difficulty. State the purpose of the meeting so that everyone present knows what is appropriate for discussion and what is inappropriate. The vague statement of the subject is probably the cause of most futile discussions. The subject must be simply and clearly expressed and all ambiguous words must be defined. Some subjects at meetings are put so broadly that it is extremely difficult to know just what the field of enquiry is.

Then throughout the discussion there must be order. This does not necessarily imply great formality; in fact in small discussion groups formality would be entirely out of place. Order does require, though, that only one person talks at a time and that each member be consistently courteous. Some definite procedure must be followed as I have already indicated, otherwise the discussion wanders too far afield. Every member must co-operate. If each person insists on having his or her own way the discussion will get nowhere. Members of the group must have a willingness to discuss points of view other than their own and there must be some agreement to compromise. There are no doubt occasions when compromise is neither desirable nor possible but reasonable compromise should always be the objective. The more each member knows about the other members the more they will be able to judge the value of their remarks and the better they will be able to secure the approval of their own.

As a leader of any discussion you should always:

(a) prepare a time table;
(b) outline a clear introd tion

(c) know the final objective;

(d) know the intermediate objectives;

(e) frame appropriate questions; and

(f) quote any relevant case examples.

For the ordinary member of a discussion group you must learn that while if you keep quiet, you will learn a good deal, you will not thereby help solve the problem. Develop, therefore, the ability to present your ideas clearly and tactfully and learn to bring them in at the most strategic time. Don't delight in scoring points off your colleagues—a committee meeting or discussion group is not a game. And always do your homework first.

Briefing Sessions

Briefing sessions are a systematic and checkable method of downward communication involving managers and supervisors at all levels. All of those who are intimately concerned with time spent in the Services know what 'de-briefing' groups are and the principle holds good in an industrial situation. They bring people together in small groups under their immediate boss in order that any situation can be example to them face to face. Consequently they, in their turn, are able to ask questions and so understand not only what is happening but why. They help keep everyone in the picture and are ideal in a scattered organization.

The key person in explaining management's point of view is the immediate supervisor, and while it takes supervisors' time, it is necessary for it to pay dividends. By using supervisors to explain management policies the supervisor is made a more effective boss, because he who communicates is he who leads. At a time when more and more supervisors are joining trade unions it is essential to bring home to them, whether or not a union represents them to negotiate conditions of employment, that this in no way affects their vital role as the first line of management.

The items for briefing are those which affect a man's will to work effectively. They will therefore be items about the job-quality, safety, changes, progress, performance of the group; and those things which affect all workers personally—promotion, employment policies, security, and so on.

Normally a form is given to each supervisor with the items to be briefed printed clearly thereon with a space left each item for a note of any points which the briefer must especially emphasize. Briefing should not only be checkable but be checked which is best done by managers sitting in now and then on a briefing session. Briefing sessions should take place with no fewer than six nor more than twenty persons present. This greatly facilitates the number of questions and answers which can be handled during the session.

More and more large companies are using briefing sessions to inform their workers of matters effecting their work and are very complimentary of the results being obtained.

Points for Discussion

o what points would you give attention before calling a meeting of supervisors to discuss increased measures for safety in your particular factory?

What rules do you consider to be important in running a meeting?

Do you consider it essential that all members speak at a committee meeting?

What is the value of sub-committees?

What various types of situation can you think of where the application of a discussion group would be helpful?

4

Public Relations and the Firm

Like inflation accounting, public relations is easier to define by saying what it isn't rather than what it is.

Public relations, therefore, is not:

A letter from a finance company saying, 'I'm a computer and I'd like to say hello';

A press release 'Plans are in hand for the replacement of the Stock Exchange film, My Word is My Bond, which is now out of date';

A statement by the chairman of a public company at their annual meeting revealing, 'The major event of the year was the appointment of a new managing director. As a substantial shareholder, I would say the company is to be congratulate on its good fortune. As his father I commend him to your indulgence'.

Public relations pace the Duchess, is helping everybody to mind everybody ele's business in order to make the world go round a deal faster than it does at the moment. In other words, PR is communications; communications is participation; and participation means progress.

There are, of course, plenty of other definitions.

The Institute of Public Relations maintains that PR is 'the deliberate, planned and sustained effort to establish and maintain mutual understanding between an organization and it publics'. Herbert M. Baus claims it is a combination of 'philosophy, sociology, economics, language, psychology, journalism, communication and other knowledges into a system of human understanding'. For my money, in spite of so much evidence suggesting it merely Dale Carnegie writ large, I believe public relations means goodwill. And goodwill is an asset to be maintained and developed just the same as any other major asset of a business.

As such, therefore, public relations can profit every single division—or activity—of a company. It is not exclusively the preserve of the scales division. Nor is it simply aimed at the mass media. Public relations is a total company service, capable of using every communications means at its disposal, to maximize that most intangible of all assets: goodwill. For, like it or not, it is now an irrevocable fact of commercial life that no person, let alone a public company, is an island. Every individual and every corporate body has its relationships and responsibilities. And the power of public opinion exists to hammer them into submission. In other words a company should behave like a good citizen in business.

Public, relation, therefore, is the corporate discipiine which ensures not only that a company behaves like a good citizen and —and this is natural for a commercial organisation—the company is seen to be acting like a gnod citizen and obtains the necessary recognition for it. After all, when John D. Rockefeller started handing out pennies to the kids in Central Park he took a photographer with him!

The public relations practitioner, therefore, trades a dangerous yet vitally important path in commercial life to-day. For while he must be a good and happy member of the corporate team, he must continually remind his colleagues of their relationship with the outside world. In other words, he is a cross between a consumer's advocate and a devil's advocate.

Public Relations and General Management

Don't let us beat about the bush. The public limited company is in business to make a profit. There is nothing wrong about that. A profitable company is an asset to everybody involved. What counts, however, is the way in which it makes its money. The profit from slave-trading might have been substantial, but it was still wrong.

The public relations oriented company will aim to strike the right balance between is shareholders, its employees, its customers and the public at large for two reasons. First, because it is so obviously the right thing to do, and the second, because the public generally will no longer tolerate any activities to the contrary—and it is dangerous for any commercial organization to go against the public will.

Public Relations and a Company's Financial Relations

The Stock Exchange,The Takeover Panel, this and that Company Law; every day there are more and more regulations governing the financial relations of a company. Just as companies have a duty to the general public, they also have a duty to their own shareholders and the investing public generally. Sir Martin Wilkinson, former chairmen of the Stock Exchange, London says, 'Communications with the shareholder and the investing public generally must be a continuous and continuing process designed with a clear undrstanding of the needs of those for whom it is designed and supported by the company making the communication.' In other words, keep the market informed about what's going on.

The company won't suffer either. Such a policy will ensure the share reflect the financial and trading position as well as the prospects of the company. It helps the company's reputation. And, of course, it helps money-raising activities.

Public Relations and a Company's Internal Relations

Gone are the days of Henry Ford when it comes to internal relations,For Henry Ford used to lay the law down on employee communications. 'It's not necessary for any one department to khow what any other department is doing', he used to say. Today it's different. Participation is writ large. Professor Scot Meyers, a psychologist with Texas Instruments, claims it is in every company's interests to develop that vital sense of commitment among their workforce. Employees want more from their work than just a fat pay pocket. Hence thc flood of house journal and internal bulletins, which ensure better means of communication. Gradually, the first painful steps towards some form of genuine participation are also being taken. Quarterly report-back meetings are beginning to appear in some companies. The wraps are being taken off some of the less important financial details. Joint decisions between management and labour are being taken.

Public Relations and a Company's Position in the Community

At the lowest level, this is the world of the parish pump. At the highest, it can cover a compony's relationships with the government machine and the legislators themselves.

A company's responsibilities should start with the local communities in which it operates and range to the whole of society itself. Employees should be encourage to take part in local affairs, sit on local committees and assist local charities. On the wider stage, the company itself must be responsible completely or the social consequences of its actions and activities towards society and the environment as a whole.

At the same time it must ensure its contacts with government for two reasons. First, to educate the government to the realities of any situation. The government machine is arguably the largest single and most powerful machine in the country. Everything it does affects somebody. To let it run riot without the benefit of front-line experience is to invite disaster. Second, to ensure the company is not adversely affected by any government decision taken in a vacuum.

Public Relations and Lobbying

This is a delicate area. In the demoniac world of PR mythology, this is the neither region of coffee tables and smoke-filled rooms. In the real world, it is the simply the age-old custom of hiring an outside expert to carry out an assignment that cannot be handled by a company man.

The crunch, of course, hinges on whether the lobbyist reveals his function or not, The nearest description one can get to formal lobbying, it seems to me. is to misquote Burke's famous definition of a Party: '... a body of men united to promote by their joint endeavours a sectional interest apon some particular principle in which they are all agreed'. The definition offered by the United Stares Federal Regulations of Lobbying Act, Section 307, is no better.

> 'The provisions of this title', it states. 'shall apply to any person (except a political committee as defined in the Federal Corrupt Practices Act, and duly organised State or local committee of a polical party), who by himself, or through any agent or employee or other persons in any manner whatsoever, directly or indirectly: solicits, collects, or receives money or any other thing of value to be used principally to aid, or the principal purpose of which person is to aid, in the accomplishment of any of the following purposes:
>
> (a) The passage or defeat of any legislation by the Congress of the United States,
>
> (b) To influence, directly or indirectly, the passage or defeat of any legislation by the Congress of the United States'.

And, of course, it has been riddled with loopholes.

Supreme Court decisions have virtually deleted 'indirectly'. Solicits, collects or receives' was held to mean what it said—which was surprising. Spend your own money and you're safe. Spend somebody else's and you're in trouble.

pressure groups and lobbies, I believe, are essential to our form of government. Not only do they provide a constant monitor on the activities of the executive, they also allow different people to contribute to the particular issue under debate. But I strongly believe we have the right to know who is behind any pressure group. Formal lobbists should come clean and tell us who they are; what they are fighting for: and how they are supported. Members of Parliament, especially, should let us known when they are lobbying for a particular cause; who engaged them; and the nature of remuneration, if any. When we know the facts we have nothing to be afraid of.

There is a broad programme. To implement such a programme for a single company is a major undertaking. It is also a major responsibility. Inevitably that means society as a whole has a duty to ensure such a programme is carried out in a fair and open manner by responsible, trained and informed individuals.

Until the day the police form a special PR Squad to stand alongside the Fraud Squad, I will be accused of jumping the gun or whatever the equivalent is of seeing Reds under the beds. But I firmly believe society has a right to know the length and breadth of any PR guidelines.

Customer Relations

Ask yourself:

Who's the most important person in any company? If you believe the managing director is the most important person in the company you're obviously going to go a long way. But, take it from me, you'll never be a salesman. For the most important person in any commercial organization in the world is the customer or consumer, the ultimate purchaser of the product or service. Without him, you're dead, no matter how sophisticated the accounting procedures or management techniques.

Yet all too often the consumer is the most neglected person in the world. Instead of seeing him as the foundation of the business, he is seen as a necessary irritant to be suffered in the of profit, like the businessman who wrote to the managing director of a large chain of hotels complaining about the condition of the bed clothes in his hotel room. By mistake, back came his original letter with the managing director's instruction to his secretary: 'Send this nut the bed-bug letter!'

Of all relationships a commercial organization has to develop and cultivate, nothing—but nothing—is more important than its relations with its customers. This applies whether you are selling industrial plant on a multi-million pound scale or washing-up liquid.

The starting point, therefore, is a company's reason for being in business.

Says Professor Theodore Levitt in his book Innovation in Marketing, '. . .the object of a company's efforts ought to be to offer a cluster of value satisfactions such that people will want to deal with it rather than its competitors'. The next point we have to consider, in that case, is what the customer wants. Professor Levitt gives an example, 'Thus if you sell pianos it is obviously critical to find out among other things what people buy pianos, who they buy them for and what all the problems are in connection with using a piano.' The answers he discovers are that ' . . . Adults buy pianos but mostly for their children. The piano is not just a noise making instrument or a pleasure giving tension-relaxing contrivance;

perhaps for many buyers it is most important as a symbol of cultural elevation. They want their reluctant children to play an instrument whose presence in the house brings credit to the parents'.

But, of course, there are planty of reasons why piano sales are nowhere near as high as the manufacturers would like '... the resistance of children, the tedjousness of learning to play, the competition of hi-fi and so forth. Hence to design a better piano, a more compact piano, a more beautiful piano, a cheaper piano, or to expand the number of retail outlets for them may be much less effective than developing a faster and more congenial way of enabling people to learn to play more easily', says the professor.

Given this reasoning, which is applicable to every product under the sun, we have the rational basis for a customer reala-tions programme.

The Product

The basic product, we assume, is acceptable to the consumer, If not, the whole selling operation is a fraud. I am not saying that every product must be so attractive and so valuable that consumers cannot resist buying it. That would be absurd. Instead, I believe, every product should have a basic consumer appeal otherwise sales would be minimal and the need for a customer relations programme non-existent.

Next, the product must be pitched at the right price. Like the politician, you can convince some of the people some of the time. But a successful product must be pitched at the correct market price otherwise, again, there is no sa e and no customer relations operation. Finally, the product—and this is the first stage of any promotion programme—must be presented in the most attractive from for the consumer. The degree of presentation or packing, of course, depends on what is being sold and varies from product to product. Try selling perfume in a plain brown envelope and you'll soon see way the packaging is so expensive.

Sales Staff

This is the extension of the attractive receptionist syndrome. Basically there are two kinds of salesmen; salesmen who sell and salesmen who handle enquiries from potential customers. Clearly, it is much better to have salesmen who actually go out of their way to sell. This might sound a truism. But go into any store any day of the week and you can spot the good salesman a mile away. It is in a company's interests, therefore, to select the right sales staff and train them to their own specific requirement.

New staff should be given a formal guide to any company, its philosophy, its products or services and its maket. How often have customers been told by a member of a company, 'I don't know if they sell that; I'll have to check.' Apart from the obvious benefits of a more informed staff, it can help promote the sales attitude throughout the organization. Sales staff proper should be trained—not only in the use of the product they are selling but in salesmanship as well. This doesn't mean everybody should be a huckstering door-to-door salesman. It means that staff should be doing their job to the best of their ability. Think of the investment a company makes in a single salesman. It is foolish not to try to realize that investment.

Sales training is also a valuable safety factor, for it ensures that any sales force, by and large, follows the established selling methods. I say by and large because obviously nobody can monitor every sales opportunity encountered by every salesman. But it helps to cut down any extreme approaches.

Some companies go as far as writing out every possible sales approach and counter-approach imaginable. The scales force have to master these before they are allowed on the road. It might be midly burcaucratic but it safeguards the company from extreme abuses and guarantees a fair response to the ultimate customer.

Sales Promotion

This is the land of advertising and public relations. There are many definitions of different sales promotion activities. In the end, however, they are all aimed at presenting the product to the selected market in order to persuade people to purchase. The actual purchasing decision, however, has to be clinched by the salesman. Advertising delivers the customer to the doorstep. The salesman completes the sell.

Lesson number one is to present a consistent image to your market place. It is difficult enough trying to recall familiar names br signs. The company with a diffused image has little chance in establishing and maintaining any consumer loyalty. Having launched a consistent image the next stage is to create the 'come hither' appeal for a product. This either termed the 'value satisfactions' of the product if you're a flower of Professor Levitt, or the unique selling proposition, if you're a student of American marketing techniques. Either way, it means the sales promotion material must present the best possible argument for being the product in the most attractive way. A good salesman does the automatically when he is talking to his customer. It is a little more difficult attempting the same thing on paper to a wide audience. It is largey because of this basic problem that so much advertising is accused of talking down to people. Unfortuately, it is a fact of life that these who complain, don't like plastic daffodils; those who don't complain do like plastic daffodils

Overall sales promotion can stretch as far as sponsoring round-the-workyacht races or simply arranging taste-ins at local supermarkets.

Point of Sale

Point of sale is virtually sales promotion on the shop counter. It is difficult enough, runs the theory, to get the potential purchaser inside the store. Then once inside, he is still faced with a bewildering choice. Point of sale material is supposed to swing him over that final hurdle.

The nearer we get to the actual purchasing decision the more careful must be the actual sales approach. The different provisions of the trade descriptions legislation control the sales information. The new credit legislation governs hire purchase terms and the true interest charges being made. Both are key figures in any customer relations programme. The more enlightened companies have anticipated these provisions in their sales promotion activities.

The Sale

Now the sale proper. Everything so far as been designed to bring the consumer the actual point of purchase. Now that we have brought him so far the problems are still not over. Not only the interests of fair trading but customer relations demand he is still protected from abuse.

First, the product must measure up in every way to the descriptions he has been given. Not only is this natural justice but it also commercial commonsense since an angry customer is going to cause more time and trouble than the margin allows. An angry customer is also likely to damage the company's reputation as well.

Second, any accompany guarantee must be spelt out in full. Schreiber Furniture Centres, for example, do this admirably. Everybody buying furniture from any Schreiber Furniture Centre receives a written pledge from the chairman, Ch. S. Schreiber:

'I pledge the Schreiber Company to provide well-made furniture at fair prices; to honour delivery dates; and to refund or replace without delay if any piece of furniture is ever seen to be less than we claim'.

Which is, of course, the ultimate in customer relations. Whether other businesses follow suit or not this should certainly be their aim.

Third, any accompanying financial enquiries must be conducted with the consumer in mind. Most hire purchase or credit sales demand a credit enquiry on the purchaser. Because of the dangers of accusations about the invasion of privacy, the provision of inaccurate information and so on, it is becoming more and more prudent to inform the consumer that such a check is being made and to give them the opportunity to comment on any information provided.

Delivery

Mr. Schreiber has already made the point about deliveries. Probably nothing causes so much ill will as delivery dates. Invariably, it is difficult to be quoted a delivery date; if a data is quoted it is rarely honoured. The customer continually complains. The salesmen exhausts the goodwill he established in the course of the sale. By the time the delivery is actually made the credit supply is at an end.

Far better to follow Mr. Schreiber's approach. Quote reasonable delivery dates—and keep to them. Nothing is more likely to win consumer goodwill. The situation is even worse in the industrial area. As a country we are recognized for our failure to keep delivery dates. As a result customers turn to overseas suppliers again and again. Not only is it in the consumer's interests that we solve this problem it's in the country's interests as well.

Installation

Once a product is delivered, the battle actually begins—especially if the product has to be plugged in and switched on or operated in even the simplest way. For I often believe this country leads the world in preparing instruction books that don't instruct, thus bungling up a major area of communication.

We've all experienced the situation. There is your brand new shining product. You've probably saved up for it. It is three weeks late on delivery. And there's the instruction book and you cannot understand a world. Our you get half-way through it and get stuck. There is a technical term you don't understand and so on. Nothing is more infuriating or likely to put you off a company for life. It seems so obvious. The first thing any company should do is make the customer appreciate its products. Yet nothing is so difficult. I've even come across British companies circulating instruction booklets in French and German to consumers buying their product in this country!

Putting out an instruction booklet that anybody can understand might not seem important in the total business context but it is invaluable in the eyes of the consumer.

After Sales Service

Stories about the poor quality of after sales service are legion. Communication again often breaks down on the part of the company. Many stories are also based on the after sales engineer turning to the broken-hearted consumer with the gallant enquiry, 'What did you buy this for then. . .?' But the frightening thing is that they are probably right!

For some reason or other few companies believe in the value of a first-class after sales service. Which seems amazing. For, in my book, after sales service consolidates the first sale and prepares the way for the next.

We all know the fantastic success achieved by Volkswagen in their overseas sales territories. Within months of breaking in they seem to scoop up the sales. And the reason? They always consolidate their after sales servicc operation before they attempt to sell a single ear. If a Volkeswagen customer needs a spare part it's on the spot.

Many other manufacturers concentrate on sales from the beginning. As a result they are rarely able to keep pace with the speed and efficiency of the Volkswagen service.

Complaints

Straightaway, let me admit there are two kinds of people who complain: the professionals and the people who genuinely feel they have cause for a grievance. Unfortunately, however, both kinds can bring a company into disrepute. It is in a company's interests, therefore, as well as being natural justicc to service any complaints as quickly as possible. A number of companies establish complaints departments to deal with customers. In some cases such a department operates under a fictitious name in a attempt to personalize the service and make the aggrieved customer feel he is dealing with a person rather than a machine.

Again, different companies prefer standard letters to deal with complaints while others operate a complaints questionnaire. Overall, there are only two rules when it comes to this critical area of customer relations: acknowledge all complaints promptly and act on all complaints promptly. Give every complainant the benefit of the doubt and you're unlikely to come unstuck. At the same time one should monitor the level and subject of all complaints. For the complaints department have often been able to show up the inadequacies of any quality control procedures not to mention any basic product deficiencies.

Customer as Shareholder

The advant of consumerism coupled with the increasing democratization of share ownership has brought this area of consumer relations to the attention of more and more companies in recent years. And it works both ways. Companies becoming more eager to turn investors into consumers and consumers into investors. For in the days of bids and counterbids it increases company loyalty. New shareholders in consumer companies often receive a personal letter from the chairman as soon as their name appears on the register. Others include a booklet outlining the consumer products of the company concerned and the places they can be purchased. A few companies have gone a stage further and arranged factory tours and office visits for their shareholders. One brewery kills two birds with one stone by holding their annual general meeting at their head office which is then followed by a tour of the brewery. Some hotel groups have begun to consider cutprice shareholder weekends during the off-seasons of the year. Shareholders feel they are more involved with the company than simply filling in a proxy card at the time of each AGM. The company, of course, benefits by filling the hotels but, in the end, both sides are happy.

I have listed ten key areas for any company to examine their customer relations. The sooner they start the better.

5

EDP Systems on the Shop Floor

The attitudes of people who are unfamiliar with computers and their applications often centre around one of two areas. On the one hand there are those who consider them to be mysterious and quite beyond the understanding of ordinary mortals. This group, therefore, rejects without further investigation any attempt to explain computers and what they can do. The other group takes the attitude that computer applications are only practicable where they are concerned with the operations of very large companies carrying out highly complex and involved activities.

There is some substance in both these arguments, but they are by no means wholly true. To those unversed in electronic engineering they are naturally mysterious, but that is not to say that any attempt to gain a working understanding is a waste of time. Many people do not understand how a car works and yet they use them. Equally it is true that computers are more commonly found in large undertakings, but that is not to say that they are never found elsewhere. Such is not the case. Not only are computers to be found in many medium sized and small concerns, but even where there is no computer, time on some other organisation's computer can be rented.

The truth of the matter is that the computer is being increasingly used in business, and whether a firm owns a hires a machine, or rents time, is irrelevant. The position is rapidly being approached when even the smallest concerns will make use of computers in one way or another. More significantly, perhaps, those which deliberately choose not to use them will find themselves in the same condition as would a factory owner who refused to install electricity to operate his machines, preferring to use steam power instead.

For those in management who are going to make use of computers as an aid in their work the most important items of knowledge required are these:

1. An understanding of the way in which computers work: By this is meant not how they work in technical or processing engineering terms but rather of the ways of presenting and issuing instructions which are peculiar to computers.
2. An understanding of the scope and limitations of computers: That is, the manager must know what he can expect from the computer and what is required by the computer if the expectation is to be realised.
3. An undersranding, in clear and logical terms, of the operations involved in his task as it is and as he would like it to be: Unless he has this understanding he can not provide tne computer specialist with enough advice and information to enable the latter to translate, with maximum effect, from present methods to computerised methods. Thus many of the advantages arising from computerisation could conceivably be lost.

In amplification of these three things there is a further important point to be made. The manager at each level in an undertaking will have a more intimate understanding of what goes on, and what needs to go on and why, than most outsiders. Obviously the outside expert will, if properly chosen, have expert knowledge of a subject in general terms rather than in particular terms. An expert in production control, however skilled, cannot have that intimate knowledge of a production control system in a particular firm which is possessed by the man in charge. Together, however, they will be an effective partnership provided the manager will take the trouble to acquaint himself with what the expert with the computer has to offer. Too often managers faced with the advent of a computer abdicate their responsibilities and leave it all to the computer experts. The resulting system is usually not so effective as it might have been, and the fault is that of the manager for opting out of the exercise.

Computer Operation

The first and most important things to remember is quite simple. A computer processes information which has been fed into it in accordance with a pre-arranged plan. The information must be appropriate to the plan. If the plan has been formulated to deal, for example, with stock holding levels it would be useless to feed the machine with information about outstanding creditors. The latter is not a part of the plan in the sense that outstanding creditors are not taken in account. A human parallel might be seen in speaking to a person who did not understand your language. You say something to him but he does not react. He cannot because an understanding of your language is not a part of the plan built into his brain. A computer specialist might say that the man has not been programmed to deal with information in your language, but only in his own.

Thus it will be seen that a computer needs instruction and information. It must be instructed !on programmed to do the things you wish done to the information you propose to give it with which to deal. The following paragraphs explain this process in a little more detail starting with how information is given to and taken from the machine and proceeding to an explanation of what is done by the machine. How it is done is not a matter for concern at this stage.

Input

The information which will be fed into the machine for processing will usually take the form of hand-or type-written documents such as orders, invoices. eheques, material or parts lists. Ideally the machine should be able to take such documents and deal with them directly. At this early stage in computer development, although this is possible in a limited way, it is certainly not yet a generally available facility.

Given the original or source documents as they are called, the next stage is to convert the information contained in them into a form which the machine can understand. The two common forms are punched cards or punched tapes. The positions of the holes punched in these are translations from human readable language into computer readable language. When the machine scans the card or tape the presence or absence of a hole in a particular position determines the nature of the electrical pulse sent to the central processing unit of the machine. That in its turn determines what happens, in the processing sense, within the machine. Note also that what happens when a pulse is received is dependent upon what was decided should happen when the plan or programme was given to the machine.

The process of converting source document information into punchings on tape or cards is done on specially designed machines having keyboards not unlike those of a typewriter. The operator depresses keys and the action causes the machine to punch the holes. The next step is for the punched tape or card to be passed through a similar machine for the purpose of verifying the accuracy of the punching. This checking is very important because if the computer receives information for processing which is in the right form but is inaccurate it will not be able to detect it and will process is just the same.

The tape or cards are them fed into the computer installation and the first need, as indicated above, is for the machine to read the information it has been given. The readers which deal with cards operate by means of brush contacts where a circuit is open where no hole is present and closed where there is. In a similar way tape readers operate by means of a light source and a photo-electric cell.

In some cases the information to be fed to a computer may be output material from another computer. If that is the case matters can be so arranged that the output is in machine readable form and no translation from human readable from is necessary. It could be expressed as a situation where one computer is communicating directly with another with a minimum of human intervention.

External Store

The information which is fed to the machine must be referred to other information already within the machine. For example, if information about a payment made by a computer is fed in, it will then have to be referred to information already held in the machine and relating to that computer, such as name and address, so that the credit is made to the correct customer's account.

This kind of information is help in the external store of the machine either on magnetic tape, similar to that used in a tape recorder, or on magnetic discs. A necessary characteristic of any storage system for information is speed of access. In a computer, operating at very high speeds as it does, ready access is very important. Both tape and storage systems can provide ready access, but the disc system, although more expensive than tape, is the faster of the two.

Internal Store

This is a part of the central processing unit. Before a computer can be used it is necessary to provide it with a plan of operation or programme. This programme is worked out by a programmer from his knowledge of what the computer is required to do with the information with which it is fed. The programme is fed into the store from punched tape or from cards or sometimes by other methods.

Once the programme has been fed into the machine it stays there to direct the handling of incoming information for as long as it may be required. It can, of course; be altered or erased at will as situations change.

The other purpose of the store is to hold information in process while other operations are performed. Then when it is required it can be released and related to the results of calculations as needed.

Arithmetic and Logic Unit

This is the part of the machine which carries out the simple arithmetical functions of addition, subtraction, multiplication, and division. Some idea of the speed of the modern computer can be gained when it is realised that is can perform up to one million such operations per second.

In addition to the arithmetical functions this part of the computer can also carry out the function of differentiating between negative and positive numbers. Thus if the machine were dealing with stock holding and information about a stock withdrawal were fed in it would correct the remaining balance and then, if it showed a figure which was below the minimum stock holding permitted, the machine would switch to a part of the programme which would produce a notification to that effect. Management could then decide whether or not to restock. If the balance shown was above the minimum level, no notification of that kind would be issued.

The Control Unit

This, like the internal store and the arithmetic unit, is a part of the central processing unit. Its purpose is to direct incoming information to the places it is required to go. For this purpose it is designed to refer either to the store or to the arithmetic unit, or to both, in accordance with the instructions contained in the programme.

Output

The section dealing with inut described the processes of converting data from human readable to machine readable form. The purpose of the output unit is in some respects designed to do exactly the opposite. The output consists of the results of the activity which has been performed by the machine in consequence of information fed in and the programme it has been given. The results can be produced on either punched cards or tape. They are not in human readable form except in certain very simple cases and may be held either for feeding back into the machine for further work or for later translation.

Another form in which the output can be produced is in directly human readable form in typescript. The operation is performed on a line printer which is a device which prints the output not letter by letter as does a typewriter but line by line. Some of these line printers can produce information at a speed of 1800 lines per minute with up to 150 characters or spaces in each line. At, say, 1000 lines per minute and 100 characters per line, that means nearly 1700 characters per second. Despite this the output devices described are very slow compared with the actual speed of operation of the machine.

Other devices exist for displaying output, among them cathode ray tubes, but these do not warrant attention in the present context.

Computers in Production Control: General

Essentially a computer is an instrument for aiding management control. To control an activity information is required. This the computer provides both quickly and accurately. Given these basic premises, it is not surprising to find that the problems of controlling production are increasingly soluble with the aid of computers.

There are broadly speaking two ways in which the computer can be used for production control, and these are:

Periodic Processing

This involves feeding information to the computer and receiving its output periodically. Thus events in the cycle of tasks, such as withdrawal of material from stores or the completion of a batch of parts, would not receive computer attentión as they occurred. This system of operation demands the availability of the computer only at intervals and is at present the most common method of approach. It also lends itself to time hiring with computer bureaux.

Real Time Processing

The periodic presentation of vital data to production management is inadequate where the computer is to be used for production control in a factory having a fast-changing production situation, *e.g.*, flow line production. What is needed is information about the events and their results almost simultaneously with their occurrence. The information processing system has therefore to be constantly in step with manufacturing events ranging from the ordering and receipt of raw materials through to the completion and despatch of manufactured products. When a computer is used in this way the method is called real time processing. Such a system demands that events in the manufacturing and allied departments are reported to the computer as they occur and that the computer can start working on the information the instant it is received. This latter requirement means that the computer must be capable of instant random access to its stared information. Not only that, but it must be possible to interrogate the computer at any time. These things require that the machine must be available at all times and not just at intervals as is the case is periodic processing.

Production control by computer can be designed to cover scheduling, machine loading, stock control and purchase control. Such a system would be comprehensive and would therefore permit close integration between these fields of activity. It may be desirable, however, in certain situations to handle only one or two of these areas, and that is perfectly possible.

Undoubtedly the most useful aspect of computerised production control is where the ability of the machine to establish and compare alternative solulions leading to selection of the best is utilised. Earlier it was pointed out that machine loading is much concerned not only with planning to meet delivery dates but also with devising a loading pattern which will provlde a balanced load on all machines, avoiding either over-or under-load. Where the problems of maximising capacity utilisation are most acute the computer offers an invaluable aid. The wide variety of alternatives which the machine can offer and compare in a short space of time is far in excess of that which would be possible by other means. Also the machine can be programmed to select the best of the alternatives and to issue the paperwork for implementation of the decision.

Production Control by Computer: A Typical System

An expensive item in computer operation is that concerned with analysing the problems to be solved, providing solution techniques and then programming the computer to handle the appropriate input data. This whole operation can be, and often is, mounted to provide a programme for a particular activity in a particular company using a specified computer. Such a procedure is obviously costly because it is tailor made. For this reason computer manufacturers sometimes offer a package system, structured around one of their models, which is devised for more universal application.

Such a system is that offered by International Computers Limited and called prompt. The letters stand for Production Reviewing, Organising and Monitoring of Performance Techniques.

The system consists of four stages and is designed to handle production control pcoblems as they are found in the batch production factory. The stages, which are described below, are interlooking and may be utilised singly or together according to need.

Stage I

This is the breakdown stage which is concerned with calculating and accumulating all furture requirements for assemblies, parts, raw materials, etc. The information which must be provided by production management is that concerned with demand. That is, details of orders received for products and spares, together with the sales forecast of what demands are likely to materialise in the future. In addition, the machine must have been provided with material and parts lists so that it can break down a demand for a quantity of a produet into requirements in terms of raw materials and bought out finished items.

The output from Stage I gives details of the economic batch quantities for parts to be made in the factory, together with quantities for brought out parts. The enables orders to be placed on the factory or on outside suppliers which will initiate the supply of parts, sub-assemblies and assemblies to meet the demands of customers, in terms of both firm and anticipated orders.

Stage II

This stage deals with stock control. It will be recalled that the proper control of stock is most important for the following principal reasons:

1. so that the materials and parts are available to meet the demands of customers and of the production plan;
2. so that the sums of money tied up in stocks are controlled with planned limits.

To achieve this is necessary that a management decision as to stock holding needs should be made in broad terms. The actual levels of stocks held of specific items may be required to very according to changes in demand for the products. Once the principles have been determined this stage requires an input consisting of stock issues and receipts. This may originate in stores or, alternatively, be feed-back information from the other stages.

The output will give details of stock balances with records of stocks inwards and outwards and will also provide monitoring of the information for the purpose of re-ordering within a maximum/minimum stock control system.

Other facilities which this stage can provide include monitoring the order and requirements pattern revealed in the scheduling stage, exception reporting on stock and other positions (reporting only deviations from plans), maintaining perpetual inventory system (stock-taking on a continuous system rather than once a year), analysis of cycle times, bulk issue control system, analysis of economic batch sizing and forecasting average demand, and the size of buffer stocks to be held.

Stage III

This is the factory planning and control stage which schedules the manufacture and issues instructions detailing the location and date of the work. Thereafter performance against the plan is monitored and reported.

Input consists of works orders which orginate from within the machine itself from either Stage I or II or from production management.

The stage comprises four integrated parts:

1. Forward loading (long-term).

   This is concerned with providing an outline, as far into the future as the available information permits and policy demands, of the future load situation. Thus management can be armed with information about which machines or shops will be over or under-loaded in the future and thus they will be able to make long-term decisions regarding such things as budgets, overtime, alterations in the labour force and additions to plant capacity.

2. Short-term loading.

   This part of the system handless the loading of the factory in more detail and up to about three months ahead on average. It will produce in formation regarding the parts to be produced on which shops, stating in each case the load in hours involved.

3. Works documentation.

   This part locates the works orders which are due for documentation and produces such items as job cards, material requisitions, route cards, etc. If the demands on computer time are such that the actual production of such documents would take up too much time the machine can be arranged to produce instead lists of the documentation required for each batch as the need arises. The actual documents can then be produced by conventional clerical methods.

4. Progress control.

   This section operates upon the exception principle. It analyses the work-in-progress file and compares progress with plan. Where performance fails to match plan the details are extracted and issued as exception progress reports. These reports contain sufficient information to enable progress chasers to locate the work and investigate the reasons for holdup or delay.

Stage IV

Purchase control is handled within this stage. Requirements for materials and bought out items are analysed and the machine can then be programmed either to print out orders on specific suppliers or to provide lists of requirements upon which the buyer can initiate what action he requires.

If the machine is printing out orders it selects a supplier upon the basis of his vendor assessment rating. This latter is a technique designed to assess of grade suppliers in accordance with their performance in terms of delivery reliability, quality standards and consistency, prices, and so forth.

The programme is also designed to monitor the progress of orders and to alert the buying office regarding those orders which are overdue. If desired, the machine can be programmed to print out the actual urge notes for despatch to suppliers whose deliveries are behind schedule.

Some Conclusions

This necessarily brief examination of computers and their application to production control is intended only for the purpose of providing a general understanding in that particular relatioushíp. In this and several other areas the computer is most frequently used primarily as a very fast calculator.

Should the reader wish to pursue his studies in the computer field he will do well to approach the subject in the wider context of overall computer control. The integration of information from all sources within the business and from outside, comparison and selection of courses of action, provision of information for policy formulation and decision-making at the highest levels in the business are the real functions of computers, and these are the fields which will offer the richest rewards. In any business, with or without a computer, a balance of efficiency levels within its parts is a vital necessity. To provide a highly efficient computerised production control system and yet to allow other activities to operate in a less efficient way can only lead to difficulties. Not only that, but the computerised system will not operate at optimum efficiency because other sections of the business will either be unable to provide it with the information it needs on time, or alternatively will be unable fully to utilise the information it provides.

Planning Ahead For Systems

The problem with computers is not, as many people think, about knowing how computers work. The problem with computers is about making the right management decisions. One must accept, however, that a managing director of a small company who sees the probable need to install a computer is in some difficulty, not because he knows nothing about computers at all, but because he is not aware of the management type problems involved until he finds himself up to his neck in them. By this time it is too late to make a sensible management decision to prevent his getting there in the first place.

So let us be quite clear. To choose, install and successfully implement a computer system is not a question of being or not being a computer expert. It is a question of good sound management practice. Very few, if any, companies are without their own problems and it would be foolhardy to expect a computer installation to be without problems. But sound management practice can, and often does, not only minimise the problems which will arise anyway, it can also help the computer department to make a majority contribution to the success of the company.

Perhaps the above suggests that no computer knowledge at all is necessary. There are thousands of small installations in the country operating very successfully with one or two operators keying directly in to visible record machines, perhaps supervised by an accountant, where there is just no knowledge of computers apart from "if I do this then that happens." At a slightly higher level where a staff of four to six is involved, there is an argument that someone with computer training can contribute to the well-being of the installation. Above six, the argument gets stronger to involve a computer professional in the senior position.

Computer Professionalism and Management Expertise

This leads directly to two important and related points. The first is, dees one bring in someone from outside and put him in charge, or does one train an existing member of the staff? As with so many things, there is no easy answer. An outsider already experienced and well chosen has a lot to contribute, but does not know the company or its existing systems. His relationships with the user department managers can be uneasy uneasy because he represents a threat to them, particulary if he talks jargon with which they are not familiar. They feel insecure The other approach, of training an existing member of the staff, has much to commend it because of his knowledge of the company and its systems but above all because he or she probably has some built-in company loyalty which one does not expect to find in a newcomer. The disadvantage is that if experienced subordinate staff are recruited, they may not hold him in the same respect as they would a computer professional, particularly if he is not well choson and is capable of giving orders but not managing, and there is the world of difference between the two.

Whatever decision is made, it is important to take into account the human relationship aspect of a computer. User departments commonly have a love/hate relationship with the computer department. Anything which can be done at the planning stage of a computer to win the co-operation of the user departments is well rewarded.

There are two ways in which the chances of success can be substantially raised. The first is never to give anyone the responsibility of running a computer installation without understanding that it is more of a management job than a technical task and that either some management expertise must be inhernt in the person given the responsibility or management training must be provided. In either case, management training is not a once and for all two-week course. Management training is an on-going exercise. The second is the responsibility of top management towards the installation. Making a decision to install and finding the right staff no matter how well done, does not of itself guarantee success. Corporate management must all times show a continued interest in its problems and successes. One way is through the level of reporting. Where a dp professional is given the installation responsibility in a small to medium company, careful consideration should be given to the advantages of having him report direct to the top. In larger companies the reporting level should not de lower than a senior executive who preferably should be a board member. Whilst it might be appropriate for an installation limited to two or three people engaged in payrolls and invoicing to report to the chief accountant, the temptation to regard a computer only as an instrument of financial control should be resisted because inevitably this will limit the computer's potential.

The Audit Function

Although a computer should not usually be regarded as part of the chief accountant's sphere of responsibility, many companies are now growing aware of the merits of monitoring without diminishing the actual responsibility of the person in charge of the installation. If the external auditors appointed by the company have computer audit experience, they will probably be willing to take on this supplementary task which should not be confused with the auditing of the company's accounts. Whilst a growing number of medium-to-large companies now have an internal audit function which can in various ways be developed to cater for computer auditing, it is possible that, in the accounts departments of medium-to-small companies, can be found someone witn potential to develop into computer auditing on a part-time basis. And, whilst there are relatively few known cases of computer fraud in the UK, there is little is doubt that if installations continue to be slack in their anti-fraud procedures, then the practice will grow. So anybody involved in computer audit should have a fairly broad horizon to take in any potential for fraud.

The Human Failure

It is a common complaint among computer users that the system often lets them down, whilst in fact the problems are the result of human failure and not any machine malfunction. It is a fact that the clerical procedures associated with the computer function are usually more error-prone than any operations of the computer or the performance of its programmes. It follows that it is essential to establish control procedures on these clerical operations in order to reduce the potential error rate.

But controls cost money: system development costs may be higher, testing more complex and operating costs may rise due to additional clerical and computer procedures. The problem is to balance these costs against possible penalty costs of processing corrupt information. In fact, although controls are usually regarded as a means of avoiding errors in the system, good controls will also guard against fraudulent malpractices. Errors can result in lost customers. Fraudlent malpractices can result in the loss of the company. Controls against fraud should not deal only with finance, because many of the publicly available stories from the United States show that many malpractices have been concerned with the unlawful movement of stocks and material. But just in case anyone should think that using a computer increases the risks from fraud, it can be unequivocally stated that with adequate controls, the riks are minimised. What usually increases with computers is the scale of the potential benefit to the criminal, which thus increases temptation.

Since the first edition of this book was published, the Institute of Charactered Accountants in England and Wales has produced second edition of its book entitled. An Audit Approach to Computers. Its title is possibly misleading since although it is a reference manual for auditors, what it contains covers all the essential methods of control for any installation. In outlining these methods, it happens to cover many practical points about computer operations and it is thus particularly recommended for users with little or no previous experience.

Clerical Control

There are many forms of control which should be considered, but one probably stands out above all other. This concerns the clerical control over the documents, *e.g.*, invoices, statements, cheques which are used to create input to the computer and the clerical control over the output documents, *e.g.*, cheques to suppliers, warehouse documents, etc. It can be argued that these are not truly computer controls at all since they are more the concern of the user departments. Certainly a data processing manager might see it that way. The danger is probably when the user department manager doesn't properly implement this responsibility, thus creating a vacuum in the system,

Batch processing, which was touched on in earlier is an important but not the only means of controlling input and output. Batch processing means that instead of actioning a transaction at a time as the need arises, a queue of transactions is prepared for computer processing at regular intervals. In order to break down this accumulation of transactions into manageable portions, the queue is divided into batches. A queue is a collection of input transactions, identified according to some logical rule. The purpose of batching is to provide a means of controlling the input and reducing the work involved in identifying and correcting errors. But the principle o batching allows for control totals to be identified which will detect any attempt to interfere with the documents, particularly the addition or deletion of a document to or from a batch. It will be obvious that success in the area of clerical controls will owe little or nothing to expertise in computers, but conversely will be a direct product of good management procedures.

The Top Manager

It has been noted by a famous consultant that most middle managers are controlling operations and fighting fires whilst the top manager's primary function is to think. It probably requires a top manager's attitude of mind to ensure success in a first time installation. This means that when facing up to the potential solutions to the problems outlined in the previous chapters, a 'top' manager will not merely be making decisions for the 12 months ahead, he will also be considering the needs of the installation to follow. After all, is it so unusual for parents when moving house not only to consider the immediate school for their children but the one after too?

Of course, the nature of the subsequent installation is inexorably linked to the first which is precisely why a 'top' manager needs to think in terms of years and not merely months. For instance, if the first installation is acquired by outright purchase with a view to writing off its value every five years, it would not be regarded as good planning if it has to be replaced in say, three years. Yet if the computer is a well proven model, having been on the market for seven or eight years, will there continue to be capability to enhance it in, say, three years from the date of purchase? Such a question probably calls for foresight beyond that of even a 'top' manager, but it does represent a factor to be taken into account when making an initial decision. By the same token, a 'top' manager should be aware of the slight extra risk should the vendor of a machine with eight years in the market, suggest placing an order for a machine to be released on the market the following month. Apart from no other user experience of the new machine, there will be a dearth of advice in the consultancy area. This is not to say that the opposite ends are always to be avoided but that they should be recognised as a slight risk area.

Looking Ahead

Mention was made in the previous paragraph of the possible need for hardware (and possibly software) enhancements. Quite a large proportion of existing computers have had enhancements made during the life of the installation, Management, during a selection process therefore, has to look ahead to ensure there is a good chance of an enhancement being possible without prematurely going to a new computer. Although with many of the very smallest systems, particularly the micro-computers coming along, the cost is such that a second and duplicate machine may be the right (and only) answer because such machines are not destined for enhancement capability. But when the time comes to go to a new computer, the choice may well be largely pre-determined by the decision on the first machine unless large sums are to be expended on re-writing all the application programmes and possibly setting up all the files again, *i.e.*, virtually starting from scratch.

Whether a relatively smooth change-over to a new computer is possible, or the change brings with it much chaos, depends on several factors, the two most notable of which are physical file compatibility between the two machines (or means of conversion if possible), and the language in which the programmes are written. A number of the very small machines are marketed with so called 'very easy to programme' languages. It is not always easy for a first time user to understand that the merit of this is sometimes of doubtful value, particularly since in the overall task of a system design, programming and testing, the programming may be less than half of the total. What is of major importance is whether the programmes written in the language offered can ever be run on another machine, either a bigger model in the company's range or another company's machine. Thus again there is some emphasis to be given to looking ahead. If a company about to become a first time user, has a 5 year plan for its own development, there should be a matching plan for the computer function. Otherwise the company's own plans for development can be impeded. To succeed where others have failed does not require super-natural powers. Neither should one rely on luck. Nor is a depth knowledge of computers any sure guarantee. Success in computers comes surely to those who understand how to manage and how to reach management type decisions.

Checklist For Managers

1. Do you have any in-house data processing expertise?
2. Is it clear if you need any?
3. If yes, decide whether to train existing members of staff, or to recruit externally, ensuring advice on such recruitment is obtained.
4. Consider what management training will benefit the person selected.
5. Decide on an appropriate reporting level.
6. Is there an internal audit function?
7. If not, does the size of the company warrant the establishment of the function?
8. If not, consider discussing possibilities with company's external auditors, providing they definitely have computer audit skills.
9. Consider what forms of clerical controls are necessary and consider getting external advice from people with experience.
10. Has anybody thought about the subsequent installation? To what extent are the magnetic tape, if any, and the programming language used in the machine, industry compatible?

Monitoring and Evaluation

Even if a decision is eventually made not to install a computer for the present, the results of such a survey should provide answers which will raise productivity throughout the organisation.

Apart from generalised questions which can form the basis of a survey, five lists are supplied which can be an aid before considering computerisation of:

Sales Ledger

Purchase Ledger

Nominal Ledger

Wholesale and Manufacturing Distribution

Industrial Systems

Users Problems not Defined

This book has already outlined some of the reasons why people decide to acquire a computer; it is usually to help solve a problem or problems in the business. Those problems are rarely defined. Instead, it is hoped that the problems will automatically disappear when the computer is installed. Unfortunately experience shows that the additional problems caused by the introduction of a new and strange technology can easily compound these problems, unless that is, someone has in the course of installing the computer carried out a survey and analysed the needs of the company.

Hired Help

This book has identified how to get advice and has mentioned consultants, bureax and software houses as well as vendors, all of whom will carry out some analysis. Of course, one cannot expect this work to be altruistic. Time costs money and there has to be a return on the investment. One can expect advice from a hired consultant to be independent of any commercial interest, but it is not possible to guarantee this, in just the same way that an insurance brokers's advice sometimes depends on relationships with insurance companies.

Self-help

It is a very revealing exercise for a company to survey itself before deciding to install a computer. Such an exercise need not be a complete alternative to seeking outside helf but if one is in a circular room without windows or doors, it can help one's orientation to know the direction one is facing before making a decision as to the direction one wishes to go. Too rarely do executives realise that there is a better way to do things because they are so pre-occupied "putting out fires" in the day-to-day work that they cannot spare time to consider new methods. It is this above all which causes organisations to become inefficient. There are too often complaints about the level of corporation taxes, the problems of getting staff, their low productivity, when at the same time nothing is done in the office to improve pruductivity by a critical examination of the system which so often has grown "like Topsy".

The Survey

A planned survey is a fact-finding mission.

A Survey is a means of:

Finding out the present method

Establishing the viability of any alternatives

Facts:

Find the weaknesses

Prove a need

Lead to possible solutions

A vendor trying to make a sale is likely to carry out a survey of the client's business in order to establish the facts regarding the existing system, whether it copes or not, whether it is adequate and whether it is economic. It is this survey which also determines the new equipment to be offered and that it is a system related to the needs of the customer.

Executives do not Know

It is often said that a detailed survey reveals facts about a company which few, if any, of the responsible executives ever suspected, let alone knew. The facts are there but the survey collects them together, groups them, relates them and provides a basis for analysis. It is also true that some companies have found it possible to manage without a computer after remedying the defects in their existing system revealed by a detailed survey. What is especially relevant about incidents like this is that when the same companies subsequently develop and again consider computerisation, they are then much better placed to make a success of the operation, since instead of expecting the computer to be a cure for problems inherent in the company, the computer can be applied to its natural task of doing more things faster.

The role of the computer in handling seasonal peaks more easily than in manual systems should not be overlooked, nor the reduced cost of overtime thereby. Nor should its role in reducing the supervisory effort in some areas, providing adequate computer type controls are introduced as an alternative. A comparative examination of the space requirements of the existing system and an alternative computer system may also be found revealing.

Some Questionnaires

Probably the most obvious method of surveying or analysing a business and its transactions is to prepare a questionnaire, or series of questionnaires, the first of which should characterise the company, capital employed, profits, number of staff, growth etc. The subsequent questionnaires should relate to the day-to-day operations which record revenue, expenditure, etc. One technique which aids the collection of the required data is the acquisition of forms used in the company. These can be used in order to enter specimen values or other information. This alone often reveals headings for data no longer used which have remained in ths system because of the effort involved in devising new forms.

Eliminate Obsolete Forms

When all the legitimate forms have been collected together, there will almost certainly be others still in the system and possibly still being completed but which no longer serve any useful purpose. So for each form a note should be made in the nature of one or two sentences which describes its purpose.

Identify the Source

The next operation which can also be revealing is to establish both the source or sources of the information on each form and who are the recipients, specifically each recipient where several copies are made. Very often two copies are filed away for apparently different purposes but examination will reveal that one will suffice. It is not only the cost of making the unwanted copy which is relevant; it is the cost of the labour in filing it and of the space taken up. One of the most common justifications for multiple file copies is the declared need for one in an alphabetic file; another in a code sequence, perhaps yet another in a day file. A computer, if introduced, can usually provide an easy means of finding a single file copy, regardless of the key available. Office space grows more expensive every year. It is conserved by better filing methods.

How Generated

The method of generating each from comes next, that is what type of machine or machines, if any, are used in the operation.

There is a very high chance indeed of a change in form dimension should an application be subsequently placed on a computer. It is therefore important to note ancilliary operations using folding and enveloping machines which may be affected by a change in dimensions.

How Many

The number of forms used such as invoices or requisitions is critically important along with definitions of the average use and peak use and how frequently the peaks occur. When a firm decision is made to go ahead with a computer installation, it is best to switch over in a controlled manner so that stationery clerks have not as a matter of routine ordered another two years' supply of forms for the obsolete system. The introduction of a computer can provide a unique opportunity to reduce unit stationery costs. This is not necessarily the same as overall stationery costs but the cost per client/per transaction. This should not be missed in view of rising costs of stationery.

Proof of Accuracy

Finally, the survey should record what method of proof of accuracy is used to validate the transactions. This means the establishment of:

How the entries, the totals, the balances, are proved?

How often?

What is the present level of accuracy?

How much time is spent in finding the differences?

What controls are there?

There are many aspects of simple systems which have little or no method of proof at all. Although computers are often said in the popular press to be the subject to frauds, it is incontestable that computers do offer much better methods of control than manual or mechanised methods of handling. If the existing methods of proof are outlined, where they exist at all, it will help when it moves to the stage of designing a computer system.

Existing methods must either be reproduced or improved methods introduced. Where no method exists, it will often be found possible to include appropriate procedures on a computer usually at no cost at all.

Ask Why!

The purpose of a survey is to attempt to see the system as a whole and then to identify the problem areas within the system. To do this, one must adopt a challenging attitude with a determination to say WHY to everything, particularly those things which are carried out in a certain way because they have always been carried out this way. This is not an answer at all and if given must be challenged with "Why is it carried out at all?.'

Facts versus Opinions

The art of a successful survey and the subsequent analysis of the answers depends very much on obtaining facts and not relying on opinions or as a minimum separating facts from opinions. At the same time one should not miss the opportunity of obtaining staff and managers' opinions on the shortcomings of the existing system. All the facts must then be critically considered in turn along the following lines.

What is done, *i.e.*, what is its purpose?

Where is it done, *i,e.*, in what place?

When is it done, *i.e.*, in what sequence?

Who does it, *i.e.*, what person/department?

How is it done, *i.e.*, what are the means?

The answers to these questions should provide the facts:

The Reasons

A further series of questions can then be put, the answers to which may often cross the boundary into opinion. These questions involve seeking the reasons behind the job.

Why is it done?

Why is it done there?

Why is it done then?

Why is it done by that person/department?

Why is it done that way?

Seek Alternatives

Further probing questions can then be put, the answers to which may stray further into the field of opinion. These seek alternatives.

Can it be eliminated?

Can it be done elsewhere?

Can it be done another time?

Can it be done by someone else?

Can it be done another way?

New System

An analysis should provide some answers to questions which create a possible basis for a new system.

Should it be eliminated?

Where should it be done?

When should it be done?

Who should it be done by?

How should it be done?

Integration and Simplification

Although the purpose of the exercise should be to eliminate unnecessary jobs or to integrate or simplify jobs, care should be taken against the dismantling of controls which are an essential part of the management system particularly against errors in payments, stock movements or fraudulent use thereof.

Sales Ledger Application

Where computerisation of the Sales Ledgers is contemplated, answers to the following questions will provide a good basis for discussions with the vendor.

How many Sales Ledgers are there?

How many Open Item accounts, if any?

How many Balance Brought Forward accounts?

How many Statement Addresses?

Are Remittance Advices required?

What is maximum size of account numbers?

What is maximum value of any transaction?

How many Invoice Addresses?

How many Invoices are produced daily/weekly?

How many forward dated Invoices?

How many cancelled Invoices?

How many Credit Notes?

How many Journal Debits?

How many Journal Credits?

What is volume of cash to Account?

Cash to Suspense?

Cash from Suspense?

How many new accounts?

How many amendments to files?

What is the average time an Invoice remains outstanding?

Are Ledger Balances aged?

If a computer is introduced, what print-outs are required and how frequently; *e.g.*

Input Audit

Transaction Analysis

File Control

VAT Reconciliation and Summary

Statements

Credit Limit and Aged Balances

VAT Quarterly Summary

Year-End Balances

What other information needs to be held; *e.g.*

Sales Year-to-Date

Payments Year-to-Date

VAT Year-to-Date

Credit Limits

Date of Last Payment

Amount of Last Payment

Purchase Ledger Application

Where computerisation of the Purchase Ledgers is contemplated, answers to the following questions will provide a good basis for discussions with the vendor.

How many Purchase Ledgers are there?

How many accounts?

How many bank addresses?

How many accounts are paid by cash/cheque?

How many accounts are paid by Credit Transfer?

How many accounts are paid by Direct Debit?

What is maximum size of account numbers?

What is maximum value of any transaction?

What is maximum value of any payment?

Are Remittance Advices required?

How many Invoices are received daily/weekly?

How many Credit Notes?

How many Journal Debits?

How many Journal Credits?

How many payments are withheld?

How many payments are released?

How many new accounts?

How many amendments to file?

What is average time an Invoice remains outstanding?

Are Ledger Balances aged?

If a computer is introduced, what print-outs are required and how frequently, *e.g.*

Input Reconciliation

Transaction Analysis

File Control

VAT Reconciliation and Summary

Payments Due

Remittance Advice

Cheques

Credit Transfers

What other information needs to be held, *e.g.*

Purchase Year-to-Date

Payments Year-to-Date

VAT Year-to-Date

Date of Last Transaction

Date of Last Payment

Amount of Last Payment

Nominal Ledger Application

Where computerisation of the Nominal Ledgers is contemplated, answers to the following questions will provide a good basis for discussions with the vendor.

How many Nominal Ledgers are there?

How many accounts?

What is maximum size of account numbers?

What is maximum value of any transaction?

What is maximum value of account balance?

How many periods are retained?

How many direct entry transactions are there?

How mony direct entry journal debit entries are there?

How many direct entry journal credit entries are there?

How many new accounts?

If a computer is introduced, what print-outs are required and how frequently, *e.g.*

Input Reconciliation

Schedule of Accounts with balances and budget comparisons

Wholesale and Manufacturing Distribution

If you are in the Wholesale and Manufacturing Distribution business and computerisation is contemplated, answers to the following questions will provide a good basis for discussions with the vendor.

In the current system, what type of numbering system is used:

Customer number, maximum characters numeric/alpha?

Supplier number, maximum characters numeric/alpha?

Stock item number, maximum characters numerie/alpha?

Bin location number, maximum characters numeric/alpha?

Invoice number, maximum characters numeric/alpha?

Are check digits used?

If so, what modules?

Describe with examples of documents along with any special reports or analyses produced the system used to produce:

Order processing

Stock control

Invoicing

Warehouse picking

Sales accounting

How many manufacturing units are there?

How many distribution warehouses?

How many salesmen are employed?

How many major product classes are there?

How many stock items are there?

How many customer accounts are there?

What increase in customer accounts is expected in the next five years?

How many customer orders are processed daily/weekly on average?

What growth in the number of customer orders is expected in the next five years?

Does the sales activity fluctuate and if so define frequency and range?

How many suppliers accounts are maintained?

What growth in the number of suppliers accounts is expected in the next five years?

For an Order Processing Application:

How many customers orders are processed on average day/week/month?

What are peak figures?

What characterizes these peaks?

Where there is more than one distribution warehouse, give the figures again for each location:

Do customers send orders direct to each warehouse?

How many item lines per order average order/peak order volume?

Are out-of-stock items back ordered?

Are substitute items offered?

How many orders result in back orders?

What is average number of lines for a back order?

How many customers have standard despatch addresses in addition to the invoice address?

Of these, what is the average/maximum number of standard despatch addresses?

On an average day what is the percentage orders requiring the entry of non-standard addresses?

Does this percentage increase on peak order days?

Can items be despatched direct from the supplier to the customer?

What proportion of order enquiries require a stock availability check before being accepted for processing?

What is the percentage of customer records affected by changes of address, addition of delivery address, etc., each day?

Is there a quantity break system for pricing?

If so, how may breaks are there?

Is there a trade discounting by item system?

Or by customer?

Are there any other special pricing policies in operation?

Are salesmen's commissions calculated as a percentage of invoice value?

If yes, are commissions ever split?

If yes, what is maximum number of salesmen sharing?

Is there a credit authorisation limit applied for each customer?

If yes, how are these applied?

How many Credit Notes are prepared daily?

What is average/maximum number of item lines for a Credit Note?

How many invoices are prepared daily/weekly/monthly on average/peak?

What is average/peak number of item lines per invoice?

Are Invoices sent with goods or by post?

Is cost and profit calculated by Invoice?

For any Warehouse Application:

How many product classifications are there in the inventory?

What is the expected number in five years' time?

When there are several warehouses, how many of the items are common to more than one warehouse?

What is daily percentage of stock records affected by change of price, or new items, etc?

Where multiple warehouse locations are involved, is the order processing function centralised?

Define the type of bin location numbering in use:

Is the inventory costed by average cost or true last cost?

How many times a year does the inventory turn?

How is inventory stock checking handled?

Are Packing Slips used to accompany despatched goods?

Is the availability of physical stock checked before a Packing List is prepared?

Is the stock reserved or allocated against forward orders?

How many stock items can have more than one supplier?

How many purchase orders are prepared daily/weekly/monthly?

What is average number of item lines for each purchase order?

How many stock item receipts are handled?

For a Sales Accounting Application:

How many customer accounts are there?

Are accounts invoice matching or balance brought forward?

At what periods are statements sent out?

How many Statements are sent in a period?

How many sales cash payments per week?

How many sales journals per week?

Are the ledger balances aged?

Industrial Systems

If you are engaged in Industrial activity and computerisation is contemplated, answers to the following questions will provide a good basis for discussions with the vendor.

For a sales Order Processing Application, state:

Number of finished product ranges offered

Number of lines per range

For each range state percentage of total sales by value and by units

For each range state current delivery period quoted

For each range state average production time required

For each range specify if the normal mechod of satisfying orders is:

ex-stock

made to order from standard range

made to order as special product without repeats

made to other as special product with repeats

scheduled orders with periodic call off

If scheduled orders, state average time span of schedules and average call-off interval

What differences are expected over the next five years?

How frequently are the forward production schedules reviewed relative to sales?

What percentage of customers' orders are late on delivery?

Are the levels of finished product stocks too high or unbalanced?

When customer orders are manufactured are the required components and raw materials held in stock?

Are customer orders "exploded" for finished products to the required components and raw materials?

Are these back-dated to provide common lead times for both components and raw materials?

Or are they back-dated with phased lead times according to levels?

State the procedure by which the customer order office notified that items have reached the Finished Product Stores?

How many schedules for orders with forward scheduled deliveries have to be changed every week due to quantity changes?

For Materials Management Application, state:

What forms of office inventory record are in use?

Do they reflect the true current physical stock position?

How many stock adjustments are posted each month to correct discrepancies?

Is stock taking carried out more than once each year?

Are the requirements for components and materials scheduled to meet current demand from customers?

Are allocations posted ahead of issue?

Can the projected unallocated stock position of an item at a future date be established?

Are issues strictly controlled by storekeepers?

What records are maintained in stores?

Are stocks classified according to turnover?

Are re-order levels set and maintained?

Are order quantities set and maintained?

Are safety stocks set and maintained?

Do stocks seem to be normally at minimum effective levels?

Are order quantities on suppliers or works determined by economic order quantity or known requirements?

What method is used to identify those orders in need of of expediting?

Is a real shortage identified only at the time an issue is attempted?

How are records of production and supplier lead times maintained?

With the present system is it possible to establish the current value of stock (excluding Work-in-progress) of raw materials. finished parts and finished products?

Are the overall stock levels considered to be too high, about right or too low?

Are parts lists accurately maintained?

For a Production Management Application state:

What documents are issued to production shops for each order?

What office records are maintained for these?

How frequently is a new production programme issued?

When a new production is issued how is work logically sequenced for operations to start at the correct time according state of current demand?

Is the forward load and work centre load measured so as to learn of possible bottlenecks?

Are manufacturing orders scheduled backwards or forwards on all operations or on first operation only?

Define how completed operations are advised to production control.

In the present system, what management reports are generated in order to assist planning and control?

Is information available on the current value of work-in-progress?

If it is rising, is it too high?

Is there difficulty in tracking the progress of production orders and the work load in each work centre ?

Is there adequate warning that excessive scarp has resulted in a short batch or an order going behind schedule ?

Are Routing, Planning, Method, Operations layouts maintained ?

If yes, state number and number of operations per route.

Also state number of amendments and new routes added.

Conclusion

The types of question listed in the several examples above are not intended to be exhaustive for any of the applications. They are intended to identify the pattern of data which can usefully be established by the company before any vendor is allowed in. Although such data is frequently not immediately available, its collection will usually identify further facts which can be added. These facts, if studied, will often provide an executive with an identification of the basic problems which had been worrying but had not been previously defined. It is the grasp of the problem which so frequently leads to possible solutions. This helps to avoid groping for solutions as so often happens, when the problems have not been defined.

For the vast range of other applications, similar questionnaires can fairly easily be prepared by a study of those provided, There is no magic about them, Too often, staff and executives have not out of the habit of asking how and why. A challenging attitude helps to arrive at the truth.

6

Information System for Materials Management

Co-ordination through Information Integration

A major handicap in supply management, as in other management functions, is the lack of coordination of activities. Many managers prefer to develop and operate separate systems and procedures for materials planning, purchasing, storage and distribution, which they consider as discrete activities. Integration of the relevant documentation is also often avoided as being complex, time-consuming and even wasteful. The fragmentation of management information resources has often adversely affected decision processes in supply management.

There is now a growing awareness that information must be integrated in view of the expanding government responsibilities and increasing complexity of public administration. To improve management processes in general, various systems methods have been developed to gather related data that are scattered at different points. This has been done successfully in some organization through the use of computers and other modern methods of data processing and analysis,

In the area of supply management. the use of computers has been found to be practicable and successful because most of the necessary elements can be readily measured, counted and described. In fact, the first commercial use of the computer was in the area of supply management, when an automated inventory control system was established in 1952. Since then, computer applications have been extensively adopted by both private and public organizations in a number of industrially developed countries. Typical computer-supported integrated information applications are illustrated briefly in Annex I.

The problems inherent in designing a successful integrated information system are complex. Thousands of details must be accurately supplied by different functions and a number of carefully planned steps must be taken toward the ultimate goal, Consequently, it is probably unwise to move directly from traditional methods into the system. More importantly, the interest, support and participation of everyone concerned in the government are vital to the successful development and implementation of an integrated information system.

Usefulness of an Electronic Data Processing System

Many techniques and methods for harnessing and optimizing information resources have been applied under different conditions. Book keeping methods and processes, manual and mechanical tabulating methods, wall charts and visible file systems are among those often used in developing countries in recording and transmitting data on materials and equipment. Many of these methods are useful but are limited in data integration, speed of processing and accuracy. Few of these methods can provide the means to forecast problems rather than to spot them after they have occurred. The application of electronic data processing has helped considerably to overcome this difficulty.

With the use of the computer, data that previously took a large clerical staff weeks to assemble can be processed and presented in minutes. Data based on computer-stored facts replace those based in empirical knowledge or trial-and-error practice. Through this technology, manual and mechanical tasks are reduced, while more meaningful integrated data can now be disseminated to provide managers with appropriate decision tools.

The benefits of electronic data processing are evidenced by a number of highly successful business applications as shown in Annex I. The planned introduction of EDP in the supply management function will not only provide more timely, accurate and less costly information on current activities but will also provide more and better-communicated data than is possible with existing techniques. The old barriers to communications and integrated systems in terms of time and distance are being reduced through the proper application of EDP. Changes in supply activities, such as long-term forecasts and plans, procurement orders , or delivery schedules, can be effected in a fraction of the time necessary to do the same work manually.

Long-term procurement plans can be developed from computer forecasts drived from various simulations involving the use of such inputs as projected orders, stock levels, economic purchase order quantities, storage capacity, distribution schedules and handling facilities. The data must be translated into machine-readable form and through the inter-action of all relevant factors; the required plan will be developed by simulation that schedules levels and frequencies of orders, delivery times, warehousing locations, inventory costs, and other supply factors.

Once the supply plans and policies have been set, the necessary control systems can be established also by electronic data processing. By the same token, ordering, expediting, receiving, storage and distribution activities can be computerized. For example, the computer can be programmed to prepare purchase requisitions to facilitate the placing of orders; it can be also programmed to follow up purchase orders, and report if the order is out of control due to discrepancies in lead times or supplier failures. In other cases, the computer can be used to determine if unplanned usage or late delivery will disrupt stock balances and the flow of materials.

Perhaps the greatest improvement derived from an integraged information system is the replacement of paperwork by organized data. Clerical processes, including tedious and error-prone computations, are absorbed by the EDP system to make more time available for decision making, planning the control. A memory system replaces perpetual inventory cards. Inventory is more scientifically planned, to enable lower stock levels to be maintained without the risk of stock-outs; up-to-date balances are produced more rapidly. Late deliveries and stock-outs are reduced. Also, cash flow is better planned.

Basic information such as data on quantities, led times, economic order levels and so forth must first he fed into the cumputer through punched cards, tapes and other input media. In addition, such variables as receipts, withdrawals, purchase orders and usage aro fed into the computer to interact with the stored basic data for the necessary compilation and analysis. The output may include inventory status reports, stock records, usage analysis, waste or loss indicators, recomputation of the economic order quantity, preparation of purchase requisitions and purchase orders, inventory investment figures, cash requirements, purchase price changes and obsolete or redundant inventories.

Limitations of EDP

Although it is difficult to imagine using any less advanced technique than EDP to optimize integrated information systems in supply management, the computer itself is not the criterion by which success is measured. It is important to know about the restraints and problem in applying EDP to integrated systems. One major problem often experienced is that the equipment is acquired without a preceding feasibility study to ascertain whether or not its use will be suitable and fully justified. In most cases, there are no trained and skilled staff to develop the systems for optimizing use of the equipment. As a result, computers are seriously under-utilized in most developing countries, especially those installed in government departments and other public agencies. The waste involved is significant considering that the cost of the equipment may involve millions of dollars.

The decision to use EDP in supply management as in other management functions must be based on reducing costs and/or increasing services, It should be preceded by feasibility studies in which all conceivable advantages and constraints are analyzed and weighed. In particular, expectations as represented by equipment salesmen must be thoroughly investigated and tested in relation to the actual work needs of the government; initial and unkeep costs must be assessed to insure that the government has the capacity to cope; the suitability of infrastructural facilities such as power supply and accommodation should be studied; and the availability and interest of trained and skilled personnel must be ascertained and assured.

Overexpectation, usually induced by EDP equipment suppliers, is probably the biggest pitfall in electronic data processing. EDP has been pictured as the panacea for management and operational ills. It can and does work in most areas, but few realize that the computer is a thoughtless tool that acts automatically. The answers it provides result from human decisions made prior to programming. The computer is not meant to be, and cannot be, creative.

Investments made in EDP are of necessity large. Equipment costs, both initial and depreciation, are high although minicomputers have brought costs down considerably. Set-up, or programming, is also time-consuming as well as expensive. Extensive infrastructural facilities are required, such as dust-free and special atmosphere conditions, storage space, fire-and-water damage prevention system and a reliable electricity supply. Personnel are difficult to find; trained and experienced EDP managers, system analysts, programmers and machine operators are in short supply. The salaries for these personnel frequently have been substantially higher than the salaries for other personnel, including those they replace.

Most managers and operating personnel have not developed an understanding of the full needs for electronic data processing. Because they do not know the limitations as well as the capabilities of the computer, they misuse and fail to take full advantage of this valuable tool. To educate the world require a complex lengthy, on-the-job training programme, which is not usually practical. Therefore, time and experience are the only practical ways for the concerned personnel to determine the kind of computer systems that are needed.

On the basis of the foregoing, supply managers will find their jobs more challenging in terms of the ability to understand and maximize the use of EDP, although they may find their regular duties easier to administer. Although the disadvantages are still evident and even more so in developing countries the pendulum has swung and the benefits far outweigh the restraints of using EDP for integrated management information systems.

General Considerations

The emphasis placed earlier in this study on the importance of supply management because of its impact on the cost and effectiveness of administration for development would be meaningless without competent and responsible officials at the appropriate levels in the government to properly plan, organize and effectively execute public supply programmes. In most governments in developing countries, the staffing of supply functions is the weakest, since the common practice is for the authorities concerned to assign responsibility for those functions to untrained and inexperienced low-caliber personnel, usually drawn from the ranks of clerical, subclerical and manual workers. Because the supply staff is untrained and in experienced, they generally find it difficult to cope with the increasingly changing technical characteristics of supply management generated by the expanding complexity of public administration and development.

The predominance of unskilled personnel in supply activities goes back to the time when the supply needs in public administration were largely limited to the provision of stationery, filing cabinets, office machines, furniture, housekeeping equipment and furnishings required to support office operations and for the unkeep of public buildings and official residences. In addition, the supply requirements of earlier periods included the provision of food and clothing, including uniforms needed by uniformed organizations and such other public institutions as the police, prisons, hospitals, and government-run residential schools.

The procedures involved in carrying out the supply work at that time were simple, generally requiring no more than clerical and manipulative skills to carry them out. As a result, recruitment to support supply management was confined to the labourer, clerical and higher clerical levels. By the same token, little attention was given to training and staff development. The low priority given to personnel and training needs has continued through the present even though there has been a major shift from the management of simple office and housekeeping services in support of simple administration to the management of complex public enterprises and other development oriented productive programmes in which governments have been assuming increasing responsibilities.

The current requirements of supply management are highly technical and demand specialized knowledge, which public supply personnel in most developing countries generally lack. Used to dealing with simple and less complex routines, the unskilled supply office: now finds himself ineffective when faced with the new challenges of supply management, which demand a diversity of capabilities including knowledge of a scientific approach to materials forecasting, procurement planning and supply-source surveys; a legal and administrative background in purchasing negotiations and contracts; shipping and transportation experience; acquaintance with international trade and related financial transactions; knowledge of materials classification, standardization and codification procedures; skills in stock and inventory control systems; and knowledge of stock-preservation techniques.

As a result of the low priority accorded by government authorities to supply activities, it is uncommon to find to developing countries clearly defined government policies and top-level directives on personnel training and staff development in supply management. On the other hand, distinctive personnel policies and special scheme of service have been developed and are being maintained for other staff and service functions such as personnel administration, accounting, auditing, administrative functions and general clerical work, which do not have as much cost impact on government operations as does supply management.

It is difficult in many cases to identify in the government any single authority or high-level central agency responsible for directing personnel and training policies in supply management. The responsibility is fragmented, the common practice being that each agency with an interest in supply activities, such as public works and public utility agencies, ministries of health and agriculture, and major transport organizations like the railway department, prefer to operate separate policies for their supply and store personnel. The fragmentation of responsibility for supply personnel policies and action has created additional difficulties. It has prevented the development of a consolidated and comprehensive scheme of service that can provide for long promotion ladders, progressive staff development plans and other attractive career programmes.

There is a pressing need for cooperation among all departments and agencies in supply personnel and training matters since supply functions transcend organizational lines. Policy-makers, line executives, staff specialists and all other concerned senior officials at different levels and in different sector of the government should all be involved in working toward uniform policies and standard rules and regulations to deal with supply personnel management. Such interaction calls for different relationships at different levels of responsibility which may be broadly defined as follows:

(a) Central responsibility for the formulation of government-wide policy and direction to be exereised by the central personnel agency or establishment department in the government, in consultation with departmental and other major branch personnel units;

(b) Action at the departmental level concerned primarily with local staffing and training needs in support of operations. This is a joint responsibility involving principally the departmental personnel unit, the supply branch and the principal materials-using branches: and

(c) Action by established management and administrative training institutions. There is a need for these entities in collaboration with the central personnel agency of the government and major user agencies to suitably expand their training programmes to include courses on purchasing and supply functions as a measure for strengthening the supply management capability of government. These training institutions should also encourage and promote the development of professional associations ~~to~~ support efforts in developing uniform standards on training, examinations, qualification requirements and performance yardsticks.

The need for recognition of sound and progressive supply personnel and training policies and actions as a critical requirement in public administration for development also requires attention at the international level to strengthen national efforts that require more support. International technical cooperation agencies can make a useful contribution in this direction through direct financial aid, expert advisory services and fellowships, or by providing training materials and equipment. Some effort is already being made but it requires strengthening and global expansion.

Personnel Requirements

The prime need in government in dealing with supply personnel matters is top-level direction aimed at establishing comprehensive personnel plans and programmes that can attract qualified staff into supply work at different levels and in all branches and sectors of government. Comprehensive and equitable schemes, including progressive career development plans, are needed to define and establish guidelines on recruitment, qualification requirements, job specifications, performance standards, training and staff development, position and salarly structures, employment benefits, a disciplinary code and other conditions of service. The new schemes and plans should be designed to cater to the varying needs of different departments, sectors and institutions of government. This is best achieved with top-level leadership and commitment which must be reflected in legislative instruments, executive decrees or administrative instructions.

Policy Directives

The policy instrument should spell out the levels of authority to be established in supply matters, and explain the responsibilities and duties to be exercised at each level of authority in relation to personnel matters. Essentially, the policy instrument should identify the central organ to be responsible, on a government-wide basis, for planning, directing, coordinating, monitoring and controlling personnel matters in the area of supply management. As previously noted, few countries have such central agencies in the government but, according to current United Nations experience, governments are increasingly becoming aware of this weakness and some have taken corrective measures. In 1969, one government issued a cabinet order for the establishment and staffing of a central government procurement and supply department. Within two years of the issue of this order, a fully staffed supply department had been established and was effectively operational.

Another government, in 1973 issued a ministerial decree for the establishment of a central controller of stores affairs as a unit of the Ministry of Finance. A subsequent ministerial resolution ordered the staffing of the unit to embrace new appointments and interdepartmental transfers. The unit is reportedly making steady progress in developing uniform supply procedures and standard specifications. A third government ordered by an executive decree the establishment of a central stores and supplies inspectorate to be responsible *inter alia* for developing a scheme of service to encompass all cadres of personnel engaged in purchasing and supply work in different government departments and agencies.

The scheme of service outlined earlier seeks to upgrade the responsibility and authority of supply management by unifying and standardizing policies and procedures relating to the functions, staffing and training in that government activity. While the scheme provides for the central direction and control in supply management, it recognizes the need for different departments and sectors of the government to maintain separate suitably staffed supply units. The guidelines provide a broad and flexible model that can be adapted to different needs. The guidelines and data are also useful for developing job descriptions to suit recruitment requirements at different levels of responsibility.

Executive Action

The second major requirement in supply personnel matters after policy requirements have been met is for the necessary staff positions to be established and suitable staff recruited. This requires action at different levels as well as close collaboration among different agencies as summarized in Chart A.

To assure that supply personnel actions receive proper and sustained attention, each supply agency or until should maintain an effective personnel monitoring service to provide liaison with appropriate personnel agencies. There are different ways to achieve this; one is to designate a departmental staff member to provide the required service. To be effective in this assignment, the selected staff member should be aware of standard government personnel practices and procedures as they apply to supply activities. Another way is to attach to the supply unit, especially to those in the larger departments, a personnel officer detached from the departmental or central personnel agency, as may be appropriate. This linkage between the personnel and supply functions is particularly critical at the stage where effort is being made to raise the image of supply management, which has hitherto been accorded low priority.

Another important aspect of the supply personnel action, as previously stated, is that there be suitable conditions to attract and retain qualified personnel in supply work. This requires that grades and salary assigned to posts in supply management compare favourably with grades and salary levels applicable to such other staff and service functions as finance and accounting, personnel administration, planning, auditing, library administration and information management. The need for this equality and comparability of grades and salary levels is even stronger in the case of posts in supply management that call for much wider and more diversified backgrounds and experience than most other staff and service functions. Training and background in planning and forecasting, market research, business negotiations and contracts, international trade and finance, accounting, shipping and insurance, customs procedures, storage planning, materials preservation, equipment maintenance, administration, industrial relations and public relations are all essential for positions in supply management.

Training and Staff Development

Need for Top-Level Support

Education, training and staff development in supply management are as critical in public administration for development as are personnel actions in the same functional area. The need for training is pervasive and continuing, encompassing all levels of personnel ranging from top executives and decision makers to clerical and manipulative staff at the operative level. The greatest need is to get policymakers and top administrators to better understand and appreciate the significance of supply management and the need for its efficient performance. The proper orientation of the men at the top would enable them recognize training and developing the skills of supervisory and operating personnel in the various aspects of supply work are prerequisites of efficient performance and cost reduction in public administration as a whole.

The responsibility for training and staff development in supply management is a collective concern as is the responsibility for supply personnel management. The range of contributors is even wider; they are drawn from both internal and external sources. The internal contributors include policy and decision makers; material buying and using agencies and departments; supply organizations; personnel offices; public service training schools and similar public institutions. Significant outside contributors include professional associations and international technical cooperation agencies.

Institutionalization of Training in Supply Management

Fundamental requirements to promote and sustain staff competence and efficiency at a high level may include the following:

CHART A

Checklist of Specifications

Nature of action	*Agency/Unit*	*Agency/Unit to be consulted*
Prepare and circulate supply personnel procedures and disciplinary code.	Central personnel agency.	Central supply agency and departmental personnel and supply units.
Define nature and scope of staffing needs. This should reflect *inter alia* job specifications and levels of responsibility; qualification requirements; duration of each post or assignment; location of work and number of posts to be filled in each grade (develop job descriptions).	Central or major sectoral supply unit, upon the advice of user organizations directly needing the service of supply staff.	Central or departmental personnel office.
Recruiting candidates: (a) announce vacancies; (b) develop and maintain a register of possible sources of manpower supply; (c) contact sources of manpower supply including labour organizations, employment centres and functional disciplines closely associated with such supply management functions as accounting, shipping and transportation,	Central or major sectoral personnel offices, upon the advice of the supply units concerned.	Buying and user departments and agencies.

engineering and construction, and trade and industry and (d) interview potential candidates.		
Induct new staff and follow up their development. Generally, this will include orientation to include the study of instructional and organizational manuals and continuing in-service training.	Personnel offices with respect of general conditions of service and supply units with respect to substantive matters.	Buying and user departments and agencies.
Monitor and evaluate work performance of staff, award pay increases, promotions and other forms of incentives and maintain discipline.	Supply units, and user departments and agencies.	Personnel offices.
Develop and maintain good labour relations.	Buying and user departments, and agencies; and supply units.	Personnel offices.

(a) Training and staff development in supply management should be pursued as a regular and on going activity; top level directives are needed to support this ;

(b) Schools and institutes of administration, civil service training schools and departmental in-service training units should expand their curricula to incorporate regular courses on purchasing and supply management; such programmes should be developed in full consultation with the central supply agency, if one exists, and major departmental supply units;

(c) Courses and seminars should be designed to meet training needs at all levels of staff including policy-makers, top administrators, managers, supervisors, clerical staff, warehouse personnel and equipment operators. The men at the top should be made more aware of the economic significance of supply management and assisted to improve their decision and management skills in that area. Equally, the subordinate staff should be trained to become suitably skilled in all aspects of their work;

(d) Staff should be released, when required, to participate regularly in all seminars, courses and workshops that may be set up from time to time. As an incentive to induce more staff to make themselves available for training, those previously trained should be encouraged to apply the new skills they acquire. The success of this largely depends upon the full support and co-operation of the senior and supervising departmental staff;

(d) Staff that have the right interest, aptitude and potenial as instructors should be identified, selected and specially trained to become instructors in supply management. As many qualified instructors of trainers as possible will be needed to multiply the number of departmental trainers required to render in-service training in supply-related activities. The existence of many effective trainers will also strengthen the resources of the central training institutions to expend their programmes in supply management training and education:

(f) Fellowships to study abroad, when considered necessary, should be planned to insure the maximum benefit. In a number of cases, fellowships for study abroad have been wasted as a result of poor planning: the wrong candidates were selected; the wrong host countries were chosen; and, worst of all, the wrong subjects were studied. To maximize the benefits to be derived from fellowship schemes, the following conditions should be fulfilled:

(i) Selection of candidates should be based on well-planned and competitive examinations;

(ii) Courses of study must be thoroughly programmed as to subject content and duration;

(iii) Host countries and the institutions where the training would take place should be carefully selected. Technical and professional competence is a major criterion; the language of instruction is equally critical. The latter requirement is important because there have been cases where otherwise well-planned fellowship schemes have failed to achieve their objectives because of language difficulties. The fellowship holders concerned were unable to adjust and comprehend the language of instruction. In some cases, interpretation facilities and introductory language courses were applied to no avail;

(g) Professional associations in purchasing and supply management should be encouraged and helped to develop. In their maturity, the professional associations should be capable of guiding training institutions in developing suitable curricula and syllabi.

They are also expected to assist the training institutions in carrying out research, developing training materials and in running their training programmes. Experienced professional associations can also provide guidance concerning qualifying standards in examinations related to supply management; develop a roster of lecturers and advisers on supply management courses; and organize and administer national and international seminars, workshops, symposia and other educational conferences on the subject. National associations have been established in more than twenty different countries and are understood to be making a useful contribution in fostering training and education in purchasing and supply management. A list of some of the known national associations is furnished in Annex IV.

Subjects to be Studied

Annex III summarizes typical courses and seminars on purchasing and supply management. The choice of any group of subject for any given training programme would depend upon the objectives and purposes of training as well as the background and level of experience of the participants. Busy top executives and high-level decision makers in government are generally available and interested in short orientation and special programmes that last between a few hours and a maximum of one working week. To be more meaningful and attractive, such programmes should embrace the following subjects:

(a) the economic and administrative significance of materials and equipment purchasing and supply, as well as the impact of that activity on national development policy planning and implementation;

(b) the integrated systems approach to supply management and the evaluation of the supply cycle;

(c) organizing for supply management;

(d) the financial consequences of import buying and acquisition;

(e) the effect of multinational sources of supply on materials standards and quality control; and

(f) implications of dependence on local sources of supply vis-a-vis dependence on external supply sources.

At the managerial level, the two broad training needs are the training of managers in supply agencies; and managers and administrators in user agencies. These require a longer time and more intensive studies in their training than the top executives. Usually, programmes ranging from one-week refresher seminars to twelve-week programme are appropriate for this class of personnel. The courses to be run at this level should include in addition to the subjects listed for top executive seminars the following:

(a) Materials standards, specification and coding techniques;

(b) Different aspects of procurement ranging from materials planning and forecasting through ethics and disciplinary conduct in supply transactions;

(c) Relevant aspects of storekeeping principles, and management as shown in Section C of Annex III. In some cases, managers of user agencies and departments may be marninally concerned with and interested in storekeeping methods where storekeeping and warehousing functions are carried out by specially assigned supply; and

(d) The subjects listed under "Personnel, Training and Human Relations" in Section F of Annex III, except that those dealing with human and public relations may be optional to the managers of user agencies and departments.

The third major group of staff requiring training in purchasing and supply activities includes supervisors and superintending personnel at the operating level. Training at this level, like that at the managerial level, should be intensive and should receive as much time as might be needed to provide the necessary knowledge and skills. The length of a course may range from two weeks for introductory programmes to nine months for the development of special skills. The requirements usually embrace specific specialties limited to different supply activities such as coding, cataloguing, storekeeping and procurement procedures. In each area of specialization the following common aspects of supply management need special attention: elements of supervision; report and documentation procedures with respect to both procurement and storekeeping functions; and materials handling techniques and tools.

Finally, there is a need to train instructors in purchasing and supply management. This type of training requires a much longer period because of the high-level professional and academic requirements that should be met. Preferably the minimum period should be six months and the subjects to be taught should include all the major elements of supply management shown in Sections A, B, C and D of Annex III, In addition, the course should cover studies in training techniques in the development, administration and evaluation of training programmes. Long-established and experienced national professional associations concerned with supply management and academic institutions should be capable of providing guidance and assistance in developing such programmes.

7

Information Unit for Public Enterprises: A Conceptual Model

ZDRAVKA PEJOVA

This article discusses the information aspect of focal points for public enterprises. According to the author, there is the need for a solid information unit which would allow focal points to effectively perform their activities of co-ordination, support, control, guidance, monitoring and evaluation of public enterprises—activities which are primarily information-based, that is, information conditioned. The author presents a Focal Point Information Unit Model, based on the concept of a cyclic flow of information which crosses at the focal point. In this model public enterprises, government agencies and other institutions dealing with public enterprises appear as both the sources and the users of data and information.

Definition of Focal Point Functions and Activities

In the same way that different developing countries have different approaches to public enterprise-government relationships, their approaches and attitudes with regard to "focal points" for public enterprises also vary. Each developing country has established its own pattern of relationships between the government and the public enterprises in line with the structural organization of its governmental activities; and this pattern defines the particular physiognomy of its "focal points."

"Focal points"—the rationale for, their establishment, their nature, role, functions and responsibilities—were most comprehensively discussed at the Round Table on Focal Points which took place in Ljubljana, Yugoslavia, in 1984. At that meeting, "focal points" were essentially defined as specialized institutions created for the monitoring, supervision, control, evaluation and co-ordination of the activities of public enterprises. As institutions which deal primarily with the nature and content of the relationships between the State and the enterprise, their attention is focussed on the stimulation and promotion of public enterprise efficiency.

The main functions of focal points can be described as follows:

to provide major performance indicators for the managerial decision-making process and a feedback mechanism for both public enterprises and government agencies;

to establish positive and constrctive interlinkages with enterprises and the parent ministries and functional agencies;

to make sustained and organized efforts toward the improvement of public enterprise efficiency.

Accordingly, the activities of the focal points are in the domain of:

policy orientation

performance evaluation

support to decision-making processes

corporate planning

appraisal of investments

inter-enterprise coordination

financial policy

technology development policy

management improvement

human resources development

consultancy

other fields.

These somewhat generalized activities are concеretely illustrated by some of the duties established in the Decree on the creation of the Secretariat for Control of State Enterprises (SEST) in Brazil, for instance;

to monitor the management of state enterprises, with regard to their performance efficiency, operations and financial and economic profitability;

to systematically organize the National Register of State Enterprises;

to coordinate the activities of state enterprises in the light of the goals, policies and guidelines of the National Development Plan. (See Netto, 1985).

Wherever the focal point for public enterprises has been defined as a basic requisite for the formulation of national policy on public enterprises, the crucial aspect of information has also been emphasized.

"It is being increasingly realized that the efficacy of all organizations, including Governments, is dependent upon the creation and updating of an information system which will provide a basis for policy making and evaluation. This is unfortunately one of the weakest areas in developing countries (*i.e.*, information systems); very few developing countries have adequate data bases for development planning and public enterprise management. It is clear that the individual Ministries, including the supervisory Ministry would only be in a position to develop data banks of a restricted nature, either on a sectoral or a functional basis. There is an evident need for a central point where data can be collected and processed in respect of the totality of the operations of the public enterprises" (Fernandes, 1985, p. 57).

In the majority of the articles and papers devoted to the subject of focal points, the information aspect is stressed as their principle role. Indeed, the strongest justification for the creation of a focal point on public enterprises is the need for a more rational approach to the quantitative and qualitative generation, gathering and processing of information—that is, for stimulating this process in those countries where there is a considerable lack of information communication, and avoiding the double and multiple expensive practices of considerable redundancy and inefficiency in data reporting prevailing in other countries.

The Information Aspect of Focal Points

The World Development Report of 1983 draws particular attention to the fact that poor data costs are very high and damaging, and that it is imperative to improve the quality and accessibility of information for management: "A good Information System is essential for all aspects of economic management. Systematic adjustments in policies and programmes, necessary in a fast changing world, are not possible without reliable monitoring of current development" (p. 71).

One of the major constraints imposed on the efficiency and productivity of the public sector has been the inadequate development of systems for the collection and organization of data and for producing information that can be used in making and implementing decisions. In this regard, many countries are hampered by inappropriate and out-of-date information systems.

The information infrastructure in general—and particularly that for data and information on public enterprises in developing countries—has not been sufficiently developed, although some countries (*e.g.*, Malaysia, Sri Lanka. Bangladesh and Pakistan) have set up elaborate, centralized and computerized information systems for the monitoring and control of the public sector. (See Ahmad, 1985; Karunanayaka, 1985, pp. 35-40, Bennet, 1986; Nawab, 1985, p. 26.)

The intensity of information communication grows almost daily, as every activity within the public enterprise itself and its every interaction with the environment uses and generates information. This constant increase in the quantity of information imposes the need for managing information more efficiently and purposefully. Suitable organization, staff and equipment are required to ensure that new information systems and services are properly implemented in the light of the broader national interests. The same applies to the information support to a focal point as well.

Generally, information may be viewed as the result of gathering classifying, recording, analyzing, storing, interpreting and presenting data selectively, in a format that is useful and timely. As the generation and flow of information mounts, information transfer becomes more and more difficult, which considerably affects the performance of the whole economic system. Indeed it, has become more than evident that information systems are indispensable to modern economic endeavours.

In order to fulfill their tasks of managing the information flows between the public enterprises and the government, focal points have to engage in the comprehensive gathering of information and data on public enterprises of an interdisciplinary nature, by creating and using a network of interrelated intelligence. Thus, they act as complex information systems which in turn require a solid informntion unit.

The Roles and Functions of the Focal Point Information Unit

The primary role of the Focal Point Information Unit would be to collect and provide information and documents on public enterprises required for measuring analyzing and understanding public enterprise performance, as well as for a continuous monitoring of the public enterprise environment at both the micro and macro levels.

A more ambitious role of the Information Unit would be to develop modelling and simulation systems which would permit forecasting and other statistiscal functions with regard to the perfromance of public enterprises and their interaction and interdependence with the environment.

In the above context the basic role of the Focal Point Information Unit would be to concentrate the information and data on public enterprises in one central place, in order to:

meet the information needs of the focal point professionals and experts in view of their tasks and the nature of their work;

co-ordinate the flow of data and information and how they interact with and support the relationships between: the public enterprises and the government agencies; the government agencies and the focal point: and the focal point and the public enterprises;

to meet the information needs of the public enterprise managers and government agency officials.

Organization of the Focal Point Information Unit

A model for the organization of the Focal Point information Unit is presented in Figure 7.1, where the source that generate data and information on public enterprise are shown on the left side, and on the right side, the same institutions appear as the users. In other words. there is a cyclical flow of information

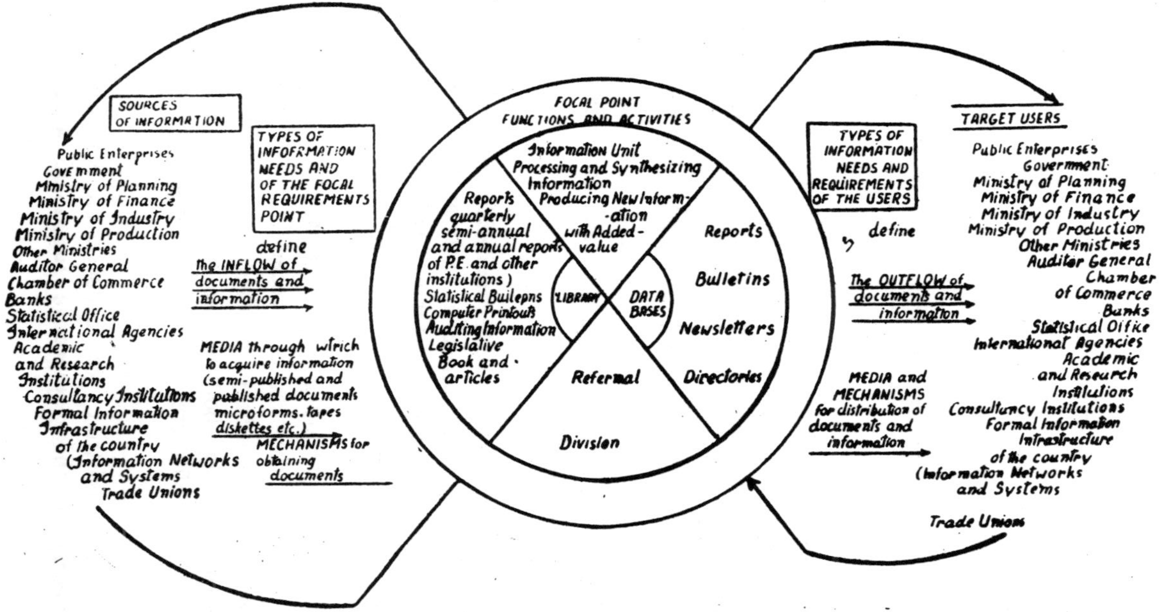

Fig. 7.1: Focal point information unit model for public enterprises

created, which is both initiated by and aimed at the public enterprises, government agencies and other institutions and oganizations dealing with public enterprises.

In any case, the organization of the Focal Point Information Unit should be based on a careful identification of the sources/ users of information, the types of information needs and requirements to be satisfied (internal/external), and of the input/ output media for gathering and distributing the information, with a view to encompassing all types of relevant information the system.

For a concrete illustration of which "information generators" and what information would be encompassed in such a system, we may use the example of the Bangladesh project, System for System Autonomous Bodies Reporting and Evaluation (SABRE). See Bennet, 1986). It includes the following:

The Auditor General: for constitutional accountablility on the use of public funds.

Planning Authorities: for post-completion audit of projects, including the operations phase as well as the construction phase, as feedback to project planning, sectoral and national planning.

Administrative Ministry: for feedback on management performance, (for decision on executive appointments and management restructuring) production, productivity (for development planning, both replacement and new projects), costs, revenues, profits, etc. (for review of pricing).

Functional Ministries: for feedback on management and policy-making in their respective functional areas. These include:

the Ministry of Industry, with respect to development and protection of industry, disinvestment, management contracts, acquisition of technology, choice of location, etc;

the Ministry of Labour, with regard to employment, industrial relations, labour efficiency, safety, welfare etc;

the Foreign Exchange control authority, with regard to foreign exchange budgeting and monitoring;

the Ministry of Finance, with regard to payments to the government, demands on revenue and capital budgets, capitalization, etc;

the Ministry of Establishment, with regard to payments and the terms and conditions of service.

Holding Corporations: for control of their enterprises.

Public enterprises are also subject to ad hoc evaluations by donor agencies, researches, journalists, labour unions, consumer agencies and anyone else interested.

Following this type of framework, the organization of the Focal Point Information Unit should be adjusted to the type of environment in which it resides and to the information needs it is required to satisfy.

The organization of the Information Unit could take many forms—from a very modest, manually handled collection of documents, to a well organized library service with documents stored over a longer period and suitably processed for easy retrieval to an online information acquisition/provision level of service.

As a specialized information and library service, the Focal Point Information Unit should consist of three divisions:

A Library Divison, which would collect, process organize, store and make available hard documents under standardized library procedures and accordingly 'provide adequate access tools to the information contained in them (statistical, factographic, descriptive). The documents collected in the Library would at the same time serve as a back up to the information services provided by the Focal Point Information Unit.

The major sources of information and documents would be:

- the public enterprises themselve
- the government (ministries/agencies)
- the Auditor General
- banks
- the Chamber of Commerce
- the statistics bureaux
- trade unions
- academic and research institutions and
- the formal information infrastructure of the country (information networks and systems).

Although the majority of documents would be in the form of reports, other documents such as statistical bulletins, studies, directories, books and articles would also be encompassed.

The Library of the Focal Point Information Unit would systematically work on maintaining and updating a documents collection of:

- public enterprise documents (annual reports, balance sheets, corporate plans, various types of aggregated data);
- government agency documents, parliamentary debates, annual debates on financial accounts;
- legislative documents concerning public enterprises, constitutional categorizations, stipulations, administrative acts,

short and long-term planning documents at the sectoral and global levels;

administrative and institutional reforms;

reports of the Comptroller and Auditor General on public enterprise accounts;

policy declaration concerning public enterprises in official documents of government parties and political organs;

all official communication between public enterprises and government which exists in written from;

reports and reviews of independent parliamentary and government committees on public enterprises, etc.

The media through which information would be acquired would be semi-published and published materials (the types cited above) as well as computer printouts/microforms and magnetic media.

It is highly important to secure the regular inflow of all these documents, which usually represents a major problem. Therefore mechanisms for obtaining documents and information should be stipulated through contracts which would oblige the "sources of information" to deposit documents to the focal point.

A Referral Services Divison, which would maintain and update an inventory of all the data bases, information system; and subsystems of information on public enterprises existing within the above mentioned institutions. It would also maintain mechanisms for directing users to the original sources of information, and thereby provide them with access to various economic, statistical and legislative information contained outside the Focal Point Information Unit. The creation of its own data bases, rosters and ditectories of public enterprises institutions that deal with public enterprises and international agencies, etc., would be another important task of this division.

A Data Base Division, with one or more data bases, which would aggregate and analyze data on various aspects on public enterprises: for example, their activities, financial performance, profitability, leverage, liqnidity, growth, equity participation, capital investments, turnovers, profitability, production, productivity employment, foreign exchange earnings, wages and salaries etc., depending on the role allocated to the focal point and the expertise involved.

A proper staffing of the Focal Point Information Unit is of essential importance. The best solution would be a special blend of librarians and information works (with accountancy, economics or management background and upgraded computer knoweldge). Acquiring such a calibre of workers has always been a major problem of the specialized information and library services in general. Maximnm efforts should be made to engage the above mentioned profiles, in order to secure the efficient operation and maintenance of the unit and its further development in response to the changing information demands of the users.

From the very beginning, the Focal Point Information Unit should orient itself towards computerization—an indispensable means of the dealing with the ever-growing data and for producing information with added value as output.

In designing the computerization of the Focal Point Information Unit, it is important that the existing standards in information be kept in view. Above all, attention should be focussed on ensuring compatibility with the national computerization policy (where one exists), and particularly with the computerization policy of the government agency information systems.

Finally, the use of microcomputer technology should be considered in the computerization efforts. This technology has made the procurement, installation and operation of data processing equipment a matter which no longer requires large investments or specialized skills. With the use of micro-computers, information and large quantities of data required for decision making at various levels or for various other purposes could be easily organized, 'processed and analyzed. Besides the standard data base, management software packages which are also suitable for handling various data and information on public enterprises are available free of charge for developing countries. (See The Guide to Software for Developing Countries, 1985). The Focal Point Information Unit should certainly take advantage of such an opportunity.

Conclusion

Regardless of the different approaches and attitudes of the various developing countries regarding the creation of a central point for the monitoring, control and coordination of the performance of their public sector enterprises, a Focal Point Information Unit would answer the undenied need for a rational and advanced means of dealing with information, which represents a critical resource and base for any economic policy activity.

The flow and processing of information which passes through the Focal Point Information Unit would not only serve to reflect the interaction and interdependence among public enterprises and government agencies, but would help the focal point to play a synergetic role in the general economic development efforts of the country.

The organization of a Focal Point Information Unit should be aimed at helping public enterprise managers and government agency officials to make decisions and carry out their responsibilities in the areas of planning, manufacturing, marketing, finance, manpower technology transfer, etc. on the basis of reliable information, in the light of the overall national economic objectives. In order to undertake such an important responsibility, the Focal Point Information Unit must be fully dedicated to the basic principles of information work; that is, it must ensure the timeliness, availability, reliability consistency, accuracy, relevance, comprehensivness and usefulness of data.

A properly designed and efficiently functioning Focal Point Information Unit would generate a series of very important "side benefits;"

it would serve to promote a common information collection policy, by requiring standardization of data reporting and information flow and by reducing the plethora of information demands in different formats;

it would prokide guidelines for clear cut procedures for recording, collecting, storing and communicating information at different levels, and thus promote the compatibilty of the numerous sources and recipients of information in the information flow cycle;

it would stimulate both public enterprises and government agencies which deal with it to take a closer look at their own information activities, and in this sense would induce more discipline in both the public enterprises and the interacting agencies to better organize the pooling of their information;

in a way similar to some national accounting practices, the Focal Point Information Unit would serve to strenghten the capabilities of a country to organize and coordinate the statistical data on public enterprises which originate from different sources.

With both the concentration of the bulk of information on public enterprises in one place and the maintainance of a strong referral service, it would be possible to avoid the great waste of time and money on multiple data reporting (performed by enterprises for various agencies), as has been the practice in some countries. In other countries, it has long been recognized that "ministries and departments should wherever possible share information rather than duplicate sets of such information" (Chuang, *et. al.*, 1985, p. 24).

It has been frequently pointed out that such an irrational practice must be abandoned.

"Commonly in the absence of a coordinated information policy, government agencies call for data from public enterprises whenever they feel the need, and tend to ask for more data than necessary, since they do not have to pay for its supply! They are not inclined to make do with the existent sources, or to coordinate their demands with other agencies so as to minimize the cost, which has to be borne by the enterprises. Consequently there is an excessive volume of reporting, a proliferation of formats even for similar data flows, and absence of uniqe definitions and classifications. This makes it impossible to consolidate available data" (Bennet, 1986, p. 15).

Information processing is a highly expensive and highly sophisticated endeavour which usually yields results in the long run and which should exclude partial solutions in principle. The initial investments are always quite high, even with the modern, cheap information technology. Ultimately, however, information processing cuts costs and improves efficiency on a very wide scale.

REFERENCES AND NOTS

Ahmad, A.S.B., 1985. "Organization. Management and Monitoring of Public Enterprises in Malaysia." Paper presented at the Expert Group Meeting on "Role and Performance of Public Enterprises in Economic Development." Mexico City (May).

Bennet, A.H.M., 1986, "Need of Management Information Systems in Performance Evaluation: An Application of SABRE in Bangladesh." Paper presented at the Public Administration Training Centre/ Economio Development Institute Module on Issues of Public Enterprises Management in Less Developed Countries, Dhaka, (August-September)

Chuang Kwing Yong, Lau Kim Boo and Tay Swee Lian, 1985, "Policy Issues of Central Managament on Government Information Systems. Republic of Singapore: A Case Study for UNDAD", Data For Development Newsletter, Marseille, pp. 18-28.

Fernandes, P., 1985, "Nodal Centres for Public Enterprises," in Essays On Relations Between Governments and Public Enterprises. ICPE, Ljubljana.

"Focal Point; A Proposal for the Improvement of Relations Between Government and Public Enterprises" in Essays On Relations Between Governments and Public Enterprises, 1985, ICPE, Ljubljana.

Guide to Software for Developing Countries, 1985. IBM, New York, 96 pp.

Karunanayoka, C, I., 1985, "Review of Government Information Systems in Sri Lanka", Data For Development Newsletter, Marseille, pp. 35-40.

Nawab, S. A., 1985, "Performance Evaluation System for State Owned Enterprises in Pakistan: An Overview. "Paper presented at the Expert Group Meeting on the Role and Performance of Public Enterprises in Economic Development, Mexico City (May).

Netto, J.C., 1985, "The Control of State Enterprises in Brazil" Paper presented at the ICPE/Economic Development Institute (EDI) International Seminar on Public Enterprise Management. Ljubljana, (August: September).

World Development Report, 1983, Oxford University Press, New York.

8

Accounting Information System

Introduction

Why do virtually all profit-seeking organizations and most nonprofit organizations maintain extensive accounting records? One answer is that these records are often required by law. A more basic reason is that even in a very small organization a manager is confronted with a multitude of complex variables. Not even the most brilliant manager can be sufficiently informed by just observing daily operations. Instead, he or she must depend on the accounting process to convert business transactions into statistical data that can be abstracted and summarized in accounting reports. In every sense, this process is essential to the coordinated and rational management of most organizations—regardless of their size. Thus, accounting is information system necessitated by the great complexity of modern business.

In today's society, there are many persons and agencies outside of management who are economically involved in an organization. These persons also require financial data. For example, stockholders require financial information in order to measure management's performance and to evaluate their own holdings. Potential investors require financial data to enable them to compare prospective investments. Creditors must consider the financial strength of an organization before permitting it to borrow funds. Also, labour unions, financial analysts, and economists often expect a considerable amount of reliable financial data. Finally, many laws require that extensive financial information be reported to the various levels of government. As an information system, the accounting process serves persons both inside and outside an organization.

Accounting can be defined as the process of:

1. recording,
2. classifying, and
3. reporting and interpreting the financial data of an organization.

Once an accounting system has been designed and installed, recording and classifying data may become somewhat routine and repetitive. While it is important for accountants to have a sound knowledge of this phase of the accounting process, it is often a relatively minor part of their total responsibility. They direct most of their attention to the reporting and interpretation of the meaningful implications of the data.

Except in the smaller business, much routine accounting work has become highly mechanized and automatic. Thus, many persons not acquainted with current accounting trends have concluded that the profession is becoming progressively narrower. Quite the contrary is true. The emergence of mechanized and electronic data processing has freed accountants from the routine aspects of recording and classifying data and has enabled them to concentrate more on the analytical and interpretive aspects of the accounting function. But these are the areas most affected by the new demands for accunting information. Indeed, statistics show that that the number of licensed accountants in this country grew from a few hundred in 1900 to about 40,000 in the early 1950s when computers first appeared upon the business scene. There are now approximately 165,000, of which 70,000 were added during the past ten years—more than the number added during the profession's first fifty years. The demand for better educated and experienced accountants will undoubtedly continue to increase into the foreseeable future.

Whether the accounting records for a given organization should be maintained manually, mechanically, or electronically will depend on several things. The size of the organization, the amount of data to be processed, the amount of information required, and the need for prompt access to stored data are some important factors to consider. At one extreme the modest accounting requirements of a small organization would not justify the cost of an electronic computer, while on the other hand, it would not be feasible to attempt to fill the extensive needs of a large organization with a manually maintained accounting system.

Regardless of the method used, the underlying accounting concepts are essentially the same. Since a manually maintained system is most easily handled in the classroom and in problem situations, it is the type that will be used throughout this book. However, where appropriate, we include comments relating to mechanized and electronic systems.

Reporting Process

The reporting process, comprising four main channels of information flow, graphically represented in Chart A.

A major function of accounting is to provide management with data needed for decision-making and for efficient operation of the firm. Although management will routinely receive the financial reports, tax returns, and special reports prepared for outsiders, they also require various other managerial reports. Examples include determination of the unit cost of a product,

CHART A

Typical Flows of Accounting Information

Management

(1)
Managerial
Data and
Reports

Taxing Agencies	(2) Tax Returns	Accounting Process	Special (3) Reports	Certain Regulatory Agencies

Financial
Accounting
Statements

Public
Accounting
Auditors

Audited
Financial
Accounting
Statements
(4)

Certain Regulatory Agencies	Creditors	Investors	Labour Unions	General Public

Reporting area governed by generally accepted accounting principles.

estimation of profit earned from a specific sales campaign, cost comparisons of alternative courses of action, and long-range budgets. Because of the strategic nature of some of this information, it may be available only to the firm's high-level management. The process of generating and analyzing such data is often referred to as managerial accounting. Emphasis on this area of accounting has increased in recent years as a result of the implementation of computers and sophisticated quantitative tools.

Most businesses are required to file many kinds of tax returns—for example, federal, state, and municipal income taxes, excise taxes, and payroll taxes. The preparation of these returns is governed by the rulings and special reporting requirements of the taxing agencies involved. Proper compliance is generally a matter of law and can be quite complicated. Consequently, many firms, especially when preparing income tax returns, retain certified public accountants or attorneys specializing in taxation.

Some companies, by the nature of their activities, are required to report periodically to certain regulatory bodies. For example, commercial trucking companies must report to the Interstate Commerce Commission, and must public utility companies must report to a public utility commission. The reported information may be used to regulate the rates to be charged (as in the trucking industry) or the rate of income to be earned (as in the case of public utilities). Although these reports are based primarily on accounting data, often they must be prepared in accordance with additional conditions, rules, and definitions. Some agencies, however, do require reports prepared in accordance with the generally accepted accounting principles that we shall discuss later. As an illustration, companies listed on a major stock exchange will submit annual reports based upon such principles to the stock exchange and to the Securities and Exchange Commission. We have therefore shown certain regulatory agencies in both channels (3) and (4) of our diagram.

One of the most important functions of the accounting process is to accumulate and report accounting information that shows an organization's financial position and the results of its operations. Many businesses publish a set of these financial statements at least annually. The subdivision of the accounting process that results in these general-purpose reports is referred to as financial accounting. Financial accounting is essentially retrospective, since it deals primarily with historical information, or events that have already happened. Its focus is on income determinaticn an financial position as an aggregate financial picture of an enterprise.

Although financial accounting data are primarily historical, they are also useful for planning and control. Indeed, a considerable amount of planning must be based on what has happened in the recent past. In andition, historically oriented financial statements are inherently a control mechanism, since they can be used to measure the success of past planning. We should also emphasize that, although financial accounting is is primarily historical, it is not merely a process of "filling in the numbers". As you study further, you will soon discover that determining the financial position and profitability of enterprises is an exceedingly complex job that requires professional judgement.

Financial accounting statements are the main source of information for parties—other than governmental agencies—outside the business firm. Since these report will often be used to evaluate management, their objectivity could be subject to question. To establish the validity of their reports, most business firms have their financial statements audited by independent public accountants. The independent auditor examines the statements and suggest any changes that seem to be warranted. He or she then expresses a professional opinion that the financial statements are fairly stated "in accordance with generally accepted accounting principles" or indicates any reservations about the statements. Usually, outside parties have greater faith in financial statements thut have been audited. Both the role of the professional public accountant and the nature of "generally accepted accounting principles" are complex.

Therefore, each is treated separately in later sections of this chapter.

Principles and Practice

To be useful, financial accounting information must be assembled and reported objectively. These who must rely on such information have a right to the assurance that the data for free from bais and inconsistency—whether deliberate or not. For this reason, financial accounting relies on certain standards or or gaides that have been developed over the years and have proved useful in imparting economic data. These standards are called generally accepted accounting principles. Since accounting is more an art than a science; these principles are not immutable laws like those discovered or developed in the physical sciences. Instead, they are guides to action any may change over time. Sometimes specific principles must be altered, while at other times new principles must be formulated to fit changed economic circumstances or changes in business practices,

Because accounting principles are based on a combination of theory and practice, these has always been, and probably always will be, some controversy about their propriety. A number of accounting organizations exist that are concerned with the formulation of accounting principles. The most prominent among these is the Financial Accounting Standards Board (FASB). The FASB, organized in 1973, is a non-governmental body whose pronouncements have the force of dictating authoritative rules for the general practice of financial accounting. Prior to the creation of the FASB, the Accounting Principles Board of the American Institute of Certified Public Accountants (AICPA) fulfilled the function of formulating accounting principles. If the attest function (auditing and independent reporting) of the independent certified public accountant is to be meaningful, the business enterprises of this country must generally observe substantially comparable accounting principles.

Various regulatory bodies, such as the Securities and Exchange Commission and the Internal Revenue Service, also prescribe rules to be used in financial accounting. Since these rules often touch upon accounting principles, compromises sometimes have to be made in financial reporting to accommodate conflicting rules and practices specified by different agencies. This has been especially true when the rules of a regulatory body have conflicted with those considered "generally accepted" by accounting practitioners.

Often, income determined by tax regulations differs from that determined by generally accepted accounting principles. When rules or methods prescribed by the Internal Revenue Service for the determination of taxable income conflict with those acceptable for business reporting, an enterprise may keep more than one set of records to satisfy both reporting requirements. Sometimes uninformed people think that this practice is illegal; actually, there is nothing sinister or illegal about keeping separate records to fulfill separate needs, as long as all the records are subject to examination by the appropriate parties.

As Chart A indicates, generally accepted accounting principles are primarily relevant to finanical accounting. In managerial accounting, the main objective is to assist management in making decisions and in operating effectively, and it is frequently useful to depart from concepts utilized in financial accounting. On many occasions, financial accounting data must be reassembled or altered to be most useful in solving internal business problems.

Accounting Activity

Accountants perform many diverse services and are engaged in various types of employment. There are three major fields of accounting activity: private accounting, public accounting, and governmental accounting Since each of these may comprise many aspects of accounting activity,, it is possible to give only a broad description for each type of accounting employment.

There are more accountants employed in private accounting than in any other field. Private employers of accounts include manufactures, wholesalers, retailers, and service firms. Depending on the complexity and size of the business, the private accountant's duties may very from routine reporting to the design and installation of electronic accounting systems. However, the major objective of the private account usually is to assist management in planning and controlling the firm's operations. In many large business firms, the head of the accounting departments is called the controller and is a key executive who works closely with other management personnel.

Frequently, a large company will have an internal auditing staff, operating under the controller or another high-ranking management officer. Internal auditing is an appraisal activity directed within the business firm to determine if management's financial and operating controls are effective and are being properly utilized. An internal auditor investigates polices and procedures designed to safeguard assets, promote operational efficiency, and provide reliable information, and reports the results to management.

The field of public accounting is composed to firms that render independent, expert reports on financial statements of business enterprises. Public accounting firms also perform a wide variety of accounting and managerial services, acting as consultants to their clients. Usually most of the accountants in a public accounting firm are certified public accounts (CAPs), holding certificates from the particular states in which they work.[1] These certificates attest to the fact that the CPA has passed a rigorous examination and has met the requirements for education and experience set by the state to assure high standards of performance. The CPA profession, like the older professions of law and medicine, has a comprehensive code of ethics—a set of rules of professional conduct—the governs the behaviour of its practitioners in the performance of their work.

The professional responsibility of the certified public accountant is somewhat unique. While the attorney and the physician are responsible only to their clients and patients, the certified public accountant may be professionally responsible to "third parties" who rely on the financial statements the CPA has audited. This is true even though the "third party" in no way contributes to the fee paid for the audit and has no contractual relationship whatsoever with the accountant.

A large number of accountants are employed by federal, state, and local governmental agencies. The services performed by these accountants parallel those of private and public accountants and may cover the entire spectrum of financial and managerial accounting. For example, the General Accounting Office of the federal government and the Department of Audit in the various state governments engage in auditing activities similar to those of public accountants. Audits may be conducted not only of governmental agencies but also of private firms doing business with a governmental unit. Accounting personnel of the Internal Revenue Service and the corresponding state agencies conduct accounting investigations of firms and individuals in connection with their tax liability. Among the many other governmental agencies and regulatory bodies that employ accountants are the Securities and Exchange Commission, Department of Defense, Federal Power Commission, Interstate Commerce Commission, and state utility commissions and agencies.

As we mentioned earlier, one of the major functions of accounting is to provide periodic reports to management, owners, and outsiders. The two principal reports resulting from the process of financial accounting are the balance sheet and the income statement. Although the form of these financial statements may vary among different business firms or other economic units, their basic purpose in the same. The balance sheet is designed to portray the financial position of the organization at a particular point in time. The income statement is designed to portray the operating results for a period of time. These financial statements are prepared at least yearly, but it is also customary to prepare them quarterly or monthly.

Another basic statement, called the Statement of Changes in Financial Position, is generally required in reporting to outsiders.

Although the balance sheet and income statement are the end result of the process of financial accounting, we shall introduce them in simplified form here, early in our study. You will find that having some knowledge of the ultimate objective of financial accounting will help in understanding the various steps in the accounting process.

Balance Sheet

The balance sheet, sometimes called the statement of financial position is a listing of a firm's assets, liabilities, and owners' equity on a given date (these terms are explained below). Chart B presents a balance sheet prepared for perfection Printers, a single-owner business, showing its financial position at December 31, 1920.

The proper heading of a balance sheet consists of:

1. the name of the organization,
2. the title of the statement, and
3. the date for which the statement was prepared.

Notice that the body of the statement contains three major sections: assets, liabilities, and owner's equity. This presentation makes it very convenient for the reader to tell at a glance that the resources of this firm total $52,000 and that these assets are being financed by two sources: $12,000 by the creditors (liabilities) and $40,000 by the owner (owner's equity). Occasionally, the right-hand portion of this statement is entitled Equities, with subdivisions called Creditors' Equity and Owners' Equity. An important aspect of this statement is that the total assets always equal the sum of the creditors' and owners' equities. This balancing is sometimes described as the accounting equation—an equation that dictates that all of the listed resources are attributed to claims of creditors and owners. Conversely,

CHART B

Perfection Printers

Balance Sheet

December 31, 1920

Assets		*Liabilities*		
Cash	$ 2,000	Accounts Payable	$ 1,000	
Account		Mortgage Payable	11,000	
Receivable	1,500	Total Liabilities		$ 12,000
Supplies on		*Owner's Equity*		
Hand	2,500	James Taylor,		
Land	4,000	Capital		40,000
Buiding	20,000			
Equipment	22,000	Total Liabilities		
		and Owner's		
Total Assets	$ 52,000	Equity		$ 52,000

the claims of both creditors and owners must be balanced by total listed resources. These relationships can be diagrammed as follows:

Technical terms:	Assets	=	Liabilities	+	Owner's Equity
Basic meanings:	Business resources	=	Outsiders' claims	+	Owners' claims
Amounts (Chart B):	$ 52,000	=	$ 12,000	+	$ 40,000

Let us now briefly explain each of the three elements in the accounting equation.

Assets are the economic resources of the business that can usefully be expressed in monetary terms. They may take many forms. Some assets, such as land, buildings, and equipment, may have readily identifiable physical characteristics. Others may simply represent claims for payment or services, such as amounts due from customers (accounts receivable) or prepayments for future services (example, prepaid insurance). As a convenience to the reader of the balance sheet, the assets are usually listed in an established order, with the most liquid assets (cash, receivables, supplies, etc.) preceding the more permanent assets (land, buildings equipment, etc.).

Assets are usually recorded at their acquisition, or cost, price. The carrying costs of the assets may be reduced for a variety of reasons (for example, insurance expires and supplies are used up). However, despite the fact that assets may fluctuate in value, accounting principles do not permit upward valuations, simply because it is often difficult or impossible to determine the actual value of assets at regular intervals in a completely objective way. Assume, for example, that ten years ago a firm purchased some real estate for $ 20,000. Today, the property may well be worth considerably more, at least in "current" dollars. Although there may be a desire to assign a more current dollar basis to the real estate, it would be difficult to accomplish unless the property were offered for sale. Most business firms do not plan to sell their long-term operating assets, but to use them. Therefore, the accounting convention of reflecting assets in financial statements at acquisition cost has persisted, although criticism is frequently leveled at such a practice.

Liabilities are the obligations, or debts, that the firm must pay in money or services at some time in the future. They therefore represent creditors' claims on the firm's assets. Liabilities are listed in the balance sheet in the order that they will come due. Short-term liabilities, such as accounts payable to creditors, notes payable given for money borrowsd for relatively short periods, and salaries owned employees, are usually shown first. Below the short-term liabilities, the long-term debt is presented. Mortgages and bonds payable are examples of long-term debts that will normally not be repaid in full for several years.

Although most liabilities are payable in cash, some may involve the performance of services. A magazine publisher, for example, may receive advance payments for three or five-year subscriptions. These constitute a liability that the publishing company will reduce periodically by supplying the publication during the subscription period. Should the publisher be unable to fulfill this commitment, the unexpired portion of the subscrition amount must be refunded.

The owners' equity in the resources, or assets, of the firm is shown below the creditors' equity. The owners' interest is equal to the net assets of the business, which is defined as the difference between the assets and the liabilities. Thus, owners' equity is a residual claim—a claim to the assets remaining after the debt to creditors has been discharged. Formerly the term "net worth" was frequently used to describible owners' equity. This expression is no longer considered good terminology. because it conveys an impression of value, and as we have seen, the value, or current worth, of assets may not be portrayed in the balance sheet. We also often employ the term capital to describe the owners' interest in the a firm. (This practice is derived from legal usage of the term.) Sometimes in economic literature the assets of a business are referred to as the firm's capital. This use of the term "capital" is avoided in accounting literature.

The owner's equity in Perfection Printers amount to $ 40,000. It consists of the amounts invested in the organization and the net earnings of the organization that have not been withdrawn by the owner.

Business Organization

The principal forms of business organization are the corporation, the single proprietorship, and the partnership. Although single proprietorships, or siogle-owner businesses, are probably the most numerous, the corporate from of business is the most important in our economy. Partnerships are often used when two or more single proprietorships are inerged into one business. For many years, professional people such as physicians, attorneys, and public accounts operated as partnerships because their code of ethies or state laws prohibited incorporation. Most states now permit a special type of incorporation or association, and professional organizations have changed their code of ethics to accommodate this change. However, most professional firms are still operated as partnerships. For large-scale operations, there are many advantages to the corporate from of organization.

The principal differences in balance sheets for the three types of business organizations just described appear in the owners' equity section. State corporation laws require that corporations segregate, in their balance sheets, the owners' investment (the amount paid for their stock) and any accumulated earnings. Because there are no comparab le legal restrictions on proprietorships and partnerships, these types of businesses do not have to distinguish between amounts invested by owners and undistributed earnings.

The following illustrations will demonstrate the variations in the balance sheet presentation of owners' equity for the three forms of business organization. Later in the text we will consider in more detail the distinctive features of corporation and partnership accounting.

Case I: Single Proprietorship: James Taylor originally invested $ 25,000 in a printing business. Subsequent earnings left in the business amounted to $ 15,000. The owner's equity section of the firm's balance sheet would appear as follows:

Owner's Equity

James Taylor, Capital	$ 40,000

Case II: Partnership James Taylor, Robert Williams, and John Young invested $ 10,000, $ 8,000 and $ 7,000, respectively, in a printing business. Each partner's share of subsequent earnings not withdrawn from the business was $ 5,000. The owner's equity section of this firm's balance sheet would appear as follows:

Owner's Equity

James Taylor, Capital	$ 15,000
Rebert Williams, Capital	13,000
John Young, Capital	12,000
Total Owner's Equity	$ 40,000

Case III: Corporation: James Taylor, Robert Williams and John Young began a corporation, investing $ 10,000, $ 8,000, and $ 7,000, respectively, and receiving shares of stock for those amounts. Subsequent earnings not distributed, identified as retained earnings, amounted to $ 15,000. The owner's equity section of this firm's balance sheet would appear as follows:

Owner's Equity

Capital Stock	$ 25,000
Retained Earnings	15,000
	$ 40,000

Any business enterprise, whether it is a corporation, partnership, or single proprietorship, is an individual accounting unit separate and distinct from other economic activities of the owners. Thus, in Case I, if James Taylor, the single proprietor, owned other businesses or participated in other economic ventures, these activities would be accounted for separately and would not affect the accounting for the single-proprietorship printing business. Similarly, the three partners in Case II and the three stockholders in Case III might have other business interests but none of these additional activities would become mingled in accounting for the partnership or the corporation.

The owners may, from time to time, withdraw money or property from the business for personal use or to engage in other buniness activities. Such withdrawals reduce both the assets and the owner's equity of the business. In single proprietorships and partnerships, withdrawals are made quite informally at the owner's discretion; in corporations, withdrawals must be accomplished more formally. The board of directors, elected by the stockholders, must meet and "declare a dividend" before a distribution can be made to the stockholders. Declaration of dividends reduces the retained earnings portion of the owners' equity of the corporation and creates a liability called Dividends Payable. Payment of the dividend eliminates the liability and reduces assets (usually cash).

For most routine business transactions, accounting is the same for all three types of business organization. Transactions that are unique for corporations are treated in later chapters.

Transactions on the Balance Sheet

Earlier, we observed that the balance sheet of a business indicates the firm's financial position at a particular point in time. We emphasized that the total assets should always equal the sum of the creditors' and owners' equities. If a balance sheet were prepared after each business transaction was completed, this equality of assets and equities would always hold true. Obviously, no one would care to do this, since the statements are required only periodically. However, it is useful for the person studying accounting to keep in mind that although each transaction changes the complexion of the balance sheet, equality of assets and equities is always maintained.

Certain transactions may change the character and amounts of assets, liabilities, or both, but have no effect on owners' equity. For example, if Mr. Taylor of Perfection Printers (see

Chart B) purchases additional equipment for $ 1,000 in cash, the asset Equipment will increase by $ 1,000 but the asset Cash will decrease by $ 1,000. Obviously, this transaction results only in a shift in assets on the balance sheet. Likewise, collection of Accounts Receivable results only in a shift of assets. Collection of $ 500 of Accounts Receivable would result in a decrease in this asset and an increase in Cash of $ 500.

If the $ 1,000 of equipment in the preceding paragraph had been purchased on credit rather than for cash, the result would have been a $ 1,000 increase in Equipment and an equal increase in the liability Accounts Payable. On the other hand, payment of liabilities reduces both assets and liabilities if Taylor paid $ 500 to his creditors, both Cash and Accounts Payable would decrease by $ 500.

Transactions changing the amount of owners' equity are of four types:

	Effect on Owners' Equity
1. Owner contributions	Increase
2. Owner withdrawals	Decrease
3. Revenue	Increase
4. Expense	Decrease

When an owner contributes cash or other assets to a business firm, the firm's balance sheet shows an increase in assets and an increase in owners' equity. Conversely, when an owner withdraws assets from the firm, both assets and owners' equity decrease. The main goal of any business, however, is to inerease the owners' equity by earning profits, or net income. The net income of a firm is determined by subtracting expenses incurred from revenue earned. Owner's equity is increased by revenue and reduced by expenses. Let us examine the nature of revenue and expenses.

A business firm earns revenue by providing good or services for its customers. The revenue earned is measured by the assets received in exchange, usually in the form of cash or an account receivable. It is important to recognize that revenue is earned and reflected in the accounting process at the time that goods or services are provided. Receipt of cash by a business does not necessarily indicate that revenue has been earned. It is true that in a cash sale revenue is earned at the same time as cash is received. However, revenue is also reflected when services are rendered on credit; assets are increased when Accounts Receivable are increased. Subsequent collection of an account does not increase revenue—there is merely a shift in assets from Accounts Receivable into Cash. Neither is revenue earned when a business borrows money or when the owners contribute assets. Such increases in assets are not earned, since the business firm has provided no goods or services.

Expenses are costs incurred by the firm in the process of earning revenue. Generally, they are measured by the costs of assets consumed or services used during an accounting period. Depreciation on equipment, rent, employees' salaries, heat, light, and other utility costs are examples of expenses incurred in producting revenue.

Since expenses are deducted from revenue in determining net income, the accounting process must relate expense in a period to the revenue of that same period. For example, January rent—no matter when it is paid—should be related to January revenue in determining net income for that month. If an annual rent of $6,000 is prepoid on Januury 1, only 1/12 of the $6,000, or $500, is considered expense for January. At the end of January, the remaining prepayment of $5,500 constitutes an asset (called Prepaid Rent) to be apportioned over the remaining 11 months. Other examples of assets that are used up over a period of time in this way are Prepaid Insurance and Prepaid Adveritsing.

Cash expenditures made to acquire assets do dot represent expenses and have no effect on owners' equity. Cash expenditures made to pay liabilities, such as the payment of an account payable, also do not represent expenses and have no effect on owners' equity. Similarly, owners' withdrawals, although they reduce owners' equity, do not represent expenses. Expenses are directly related to the earning of revenue. They are determined by measuring the amount of assets of services consumed (he expired) during an accounting period.

The foregoing concepts of revenue and expense apply to firms that employ an accrual basis accounting system. In accrual accounting, expense incurred is matched with related revenue earned to determine a meaningful net income figure for a particular time period. As we mentioned earlier, the revenue and expenses for determining net income do not depend on the time periods when cash is actually received or expended.

Certain businesses, principally service enterprises (such as law, architecture, or hairdressing), often use a cash basis mode of accounting. In contrast to accrual basis accounting, the cash basis system does recognize revenues when money is received and expenses when money is paid. Cash basis accounting is used primarily because it can provide certain income tax benefits and because of its simplicity. However, cash basis financial statements may distort the portrayal of financial position and operating results of a business. Consequently, most business firms use the accrual basis of accounting.

An Illustration

Now that we have described the basic concepts underlying the preparation of financial statements, jet us illustrate their application with an example.

Assume that A.B. Cole, a resident physician in a local hospital, decides to enter private practice on December 1 of the current year, and establishes a single proprietorship called the Cole Clinic. The transactions for the first month of operations are analyzed below. After each transaction, a balance sheet is presented so that the effect of the transaction on the balance sheet may be examined.[2]

1. December 1. Dr. Cole invested $ 20,000 personal funds in the clinic. This first business transaction results in an increase in the asset Cash and in increase in Cole's equity (Capital) on the clinic's balance sheet.

Balance Sheet

Assets		*Liabilities*	
Cash	$ 20,000	(none)	
		Owner's Equity	
		Cole, Copital	$ 20,000
Total Assets	$ 20,000	Total Equities	$ 20,000
			$ 20,000

2. December 1. The doctor paid $ 300 December rent for clinic office spece. This expenditure is an expense for the month of December. Since formal financial statements will be prepared at the end of the month, the $ 300 will be an incurred cost for services received during the month. The effect is to reduce assets (Cash) and owner's equity (Cole, Capital) by $ 300.

Balance Sheet

Assets		*Liabilities*	
Cash	$ 19,700	(none)	
		Owner's Equity	
		Cole, Capital	$ 19,700
Total Assets	$ 19,700	Total Equities	$ 19,700

3. December 1. Dr. Cole purchased medical equipment for $ 10,000 cash. The acquisition of equipment for cash reduces the cash balance and results in the appearance of another asset for an equivalect amount. This transaction is merely the conversion of one asset to another.

Balance Sheet

Assets		*Liabilities*	
Cash	$ 9,700	(none)	
Equipment	10,000		
		Owner's Equity	
		Cole Capital	$ 19,700
Total Assets	$ 19,700	Total Equities	$ 19,700

4. December 5. Dr. Cole purchased $ 400 worth of supplies on account (*i.e.*, he charged them) This transaction increases assets (Supplies on Hand) by $ 400 and results in a liability (Accounts Payable) of $ 400. Although assets are increased, there is no change in owner's equity. Instead, a creditor's equity appears on the balance sheet because we cannot anticipate the amount

Balance Sheet

Assets		*Liabilities*	
Cash	$ 9,700	Account Payable	$ 400
Supplies on Hand	400		
Equipment	10,000		
		Owner's Equity	
		Cole, Capital	19,700
Total Assets	$ 20,100	Total Equities	$ 20,100

of supplies that will be used become expense) in December, the entre $ 400 is classified as an asset. Later, when the amount of supplies used is determined, an expense will be reflected—see item (11).

5. December 15. Patients were billed $ 1,600 for services performed during the first half of December. As medical services are rendered, the asset Accounts Recievable is generated and owner's equity is increased. Note that the firm has earned revenue amounting to $ 1,600 by providing services, and that revenue increases assets and owner capital when earned—even though payment may not be received until a later period.

Balance Sheet

Assets		*Liabilities*	
Cash	$ 9,700	Account Payable	$ 400
Accounts Receivable	1,600	*Owner's Equity*	
Supplies on Hand	400	Cole, Capital	21,300
Equipment	10,000		
Total Assets	$ 21,700	Total Equities	$ 21,700

6. December 20. Dr. Cole paid $ 200 on account for supplies purchased December 5 (4). Paying $ 200 of the $ 400 owed for supplies reduces both Cash and

Balance Sheet

Assets		*Liabilities*	
Cash	$ 9,500	Accounts Payable	$ 200
Accounts Receivable	1,600	*Owner's Equity*	

Supplies on Hand	400	Cole, Capital	21,300
Equipment	10,000		
Total Assets	$ 21,500	Total Equities	$ 21,500

Accounts Payable. Both assets and liabilities are therefore reduced. This payment is not an expense. It is the partial settlement of a previously recorded obligation; no new supplies were received.

7. December 31. Nurse's salary for December was paid, $450. This amount is an expense for December, decreasing both assets and owner's equity, since the amount represents services used during the period. Cash and Cole, Capital both are reduced by $ 450.

Balance Sheet

Assets		*Liabilities*	
Cash	$ 9,050	Accounts Payable	$ 200
Accounts Receivable	1,600	*Owner's Equity*	
Supplies on Hand	400	Cole, Capital	20,850
Equipment	10,000		
Total Assets	$ 21,050	Total Equities	$ 21,050

8. December 31. Dr. Cole received $ 700 on account from patients billed December 15. This increases Cash and decreases Accounts Receivable—merely a shift in assets. Note that the revenue, resulting in a increase in owner's equity, had already been reflected when billings were made on December 15.

Balance Sheet

Assets		*Liabilities*	
Cash	$ 9,750	Accounts Payable	$ 200
Accounts Receivable	900	*Owner's Equity*	
Supplies on Hand	400	Cole, Capital	20,850
Equipment	10,000		
Total Assests	$ 21,050	Total Equities	$ 21,050

9. December 31. Patients were bslled for services performed during the last half of December. This transaction is the same as that explained in (5). There is an $ 1,800 increase in both Accounts Receivable and Cole, Capital.

Balance Sheet

Assets		*Liabilities*	
Cash	$ 9,750	Accounts Payable	$ 200
Accounts Receivable	2,700	*Owner's Equity*	
Supplies on Hand	400	Cale, Capital	22,650
Equipment	10,000		
Total Assets	$ 22,850	Total Equities	$ 22,850

10. December 31. Dr Cole withdrew $ 600 each for personal use. This withdrawal reduces Cash and owner's equity by $ 600. Note that the effect of this transaction is the reverse of the very first transaction in which Cole invested funds in the clinic.

Balance Sheet

Assets		*Liabilities*	
Cash	$ 9,150	Accounts Payable	$ 200
Accounts Receivable	2,700	*Owner's Equity*	
Supplies on Aand	400	Cole, Capital	22,050
Equipment	10,000		
Total Assets	$ 22,250	Total Equities	$ 22,20

11. December 31. Supplies were counted and $ 300 worth are on hand; this iddicates that $ 100 of supplies were used in December. When supplies were purchased December 5 (4), their entire cost, $ 400, was reflected as an asset. At the end of the period, the remaining supplies are counted and the amount is substracted from Supplies on Hand. The difference is the amount used, or expense, for the period. The result is a decrease in the asset Supplies on Hand a decrease in cole, Capital,

Balance Sheet

Assets		*Liabilities*	
Cash	$ 9,150	Accounts Payable	$ 200
Accounts Receivable	2,700	*Owner's Equity*	
Supplies on Hand	300	Cole, Capital	21,950
Equipment	10,000		
Total Assets	$ 22,150	Total Equities	$ 22,150

12. December 31. Dr. Cole estimated one month's depreciation on equipment to be $ 80. Depreciable assets such as Cole's medical equipment are used up with the passage of time. Therefore, each accounting period in which these assets are used to earn revenues should reflect as expense a portion of the cost of such assets. The amount is obtained by diving the estimated life of tee assets into their total cost, Both the asset Equipment and Cole, Capital are reduced by this amount. (We have reduced the equipment amount directly here, for the sake of simplicity. In subsequent chapters; we will present a alternative method of handling depreciation in the balance sheet.)

Balance Sheet

Assets		*Liabilities*	
Cash	$ 9,150	Accounts Payable	$ 200
Accounts Receivable	2,700	*Owner's Equity*	
Supplies on Hand	300	Cole, Capital	21,870
Equipment	9,920		
Total Assets	$22,070	Total Equities	$22,070

13. December 31. Dr. Cole estimated that the office utilities (heat, electricity, and telephone) used but not yet paid for would amount to $ 40. Since the amount of utilities used during December should be shown as expense in this month, it is necessary to estimate them. This amount should be reflected by increasing liabilities (Accounts Payable) and decreasing Cole, Capital by $ 40.

Balance Sheet

Assets		*Liabilities*	
Cash	$ 9,150	Accounts Payable	$ 240
Accounts Receivable	2,700	*Owner's Equity*	
Supplies on Hand	300	Cole, Capital	21,830
Equipment	9,920		
Total Assets	$ 22,070	Total Equities	$ 22,070

Chart C. summarizes the foregoing activities and shows their effect on the balance sheet equation. The final results are, of bourse, identical to those given on the balance sheet prepared after transaction (13). We repeat that this December 31 balance sheet is the only one that the Cole Clinic would actually prepare.

As a result of the Clinic's December activities, Dr. Cole increased his capital from $ 20,000 his original investment, to $ 21,830—an increase of $ 1,830. Had Dr. Cole not withdrawn $ 600 for personal use, the increase would have been $ 2,430. This latter amount represents the net income, or net earnings, for December.

Income Statement

Although it is very important to know the net income amount, it is equally important to know how it was earned. To show the results of operations for a period, an income statement is prepared, which lists the revenues and expenses and presents the resulting net income amount. To prepare a December income statement for the Cole Clinic, we must identify the revenues and expenses by analyzing the changes in owner's equity for the period. The changes in Dr. Cole's capital, taken from Chart C. are shown, ahead, with an explanation of each change:

CHART C

Summary of December Activities and Their Effect on Balance Sheet Equation

	Assets				=Liabilities+Owner's Equity	
Transactions	Cash	Accounts Receivable	Supplies on Hand	Equipment	Accounts Payable	A.B. Cole, Capital
1.	+$20,000					+$20,000
2.	— 300					— 300
3.	— 10,000			+$10,000		
4.			+$400		+$400	
5.		+$1,600				+ 1,600
6.	— 200				— 200	
7.	— 450					— 450
8.	+ 700	— 700				
9.		+ 1,800				+ 1,800
10.	— 600					— 600
11.			— 100			— 100
12.				— 80		— 80
13.					+ 40	— 40
	$9,150	$2,700	$300	$9,920	$240	$21,830
			$22,070		$21,070	

1. Capital contribution	+$ 20,000	
2. Rent expense	—	300
5. Billings to patients	+	1,600
7. Salary expense (nurse)	—	450
9. Billings to patients	+	1,800
10. Withdrawal by Cole	—	600
11. Supplies expense	—	100
12. Depreciation expense	—	80
13. Utilities expense	—	40
Ending Capital Balance	g 21,830	

From the above listing, we see that revenue, or fees earned amounts to $3,400 (the sum of the billings to patients of $1,600 and $1,800 in (5) and (9). The expenses are derived from transactions (2) and (7) for rent and salary, and the calculation made by Cole in (11), (12) and (13) to reflect the amounts of supplies used, depreciation expense incurred, and utilities consumed. Items (1) and (10), representing contributions and withdrawals by Cole, are ignored in preparing the income statement.

The formal income statement for the month of December, which would be prepared to accompany the December 31 balance sheet, appears in Chart D.

Balance Sheet and Income Statement

We have seen that the balance sheet and income statement complement each other. The income statement summarizes the operating results for the year, and these results are reflected in

CHART D

Cole Clinic

Income Statement

For the Month of December, 1920

Revenue		
Fees Earned		$ 3,400
Expenses		
Rent Expense	$ 300	
Salary Expense	450	
Supplies Expense	100	
Depreciation Expense	80	
Utilities Expense	40	
Total Expenses		970
Net Income for December		$ 2,430

the owners' equity on the balance sheet. The complementary relationship might be shown graphically as follows:

Dec. 31, 1910	Year 1911	Dee. 31, 19×1	Year 1912	Dec. 31, 1912
Balance Sheet	Income Statement	Balance Sheet	Income Statement	Balance Sheet

Frequently, a statement of owners' equity will be prepared to accompany the balance sheet and income statement. This is simply a summary of the changes in the owners' capital balance during the accounting period. Chart E shows this type of statement for the Cole Clinic. Note that the ending balance on this statement agrees with the owner's capital balance on the balance sheet at December 31, 1920.

CHART E

Cole Clinic

Statement of Owner's Equity

For the Month of December, 1920

Balance, December 1, 1920	$—0—
Add: Contributions	20,000
Net Income for December	2,430
	$ 22,430
Deduct: Withdrawals in December	600
Balance, December 31, 1920	$ 21,830

This statement further demonstrates the relationship between the income statement and the balance sheet. The net income (or not loss) for a period is an input into the statement of owners' equity, while the ending owners' equity balance on the statement is an input into the balance sheet at the end of the period. When financial statements are prepared, the sequence suggested by this relationship is customarily followed; that is, the income statement is prepared first, then the statement of owners' equity (when such a statement is prepared to accompany the income statement and balance sheet), and then the balance sheet.

Checklist

1. Although a balance sheet and an income statement are usually prepared at the same time, a balance sheet presents financial position at a point in time, while the income statement presents operating results for a period of time.
2. The accounting equation, Assets=Liabilities+Owners' Equity, represents the basic structure of the balance sheet and holds true after each business transaction.

3. In determining net income (revenue minus expenses) on the accrual basis, revenue is recognized when earned rather than when cash is collected, and expenses are recognized when goods and services are used rather than when they are paid for.
4. Owners' equity can be increased by contributions from owners aud by revenue. It can be decreased by withdrawals and expenses. Only revenue and expenses are used in determining net income,

NOTES AND REFERENCES

1. Most states still allow certain accounts who are not "certified" to practice public accounting.
2. The totals in the various financial statements shown in this chapter have been double-ruled. Accountants do this principally to signify that all necessary calculations have been perforned and to emphasize final amounts for the benefit of readers. We shall also employ double rulings in various other accounting records and forms illustrated in this text for the reasons given and also to separate certain recorded data by time periods.

9

*Information Technology**

I

The speed and dimensions of technological development have assumed such proportions that it is almost necessary to assume a certain amount of common knowledge about computers and related technologies. Computer Literacy has become as important as one can say the three 'R's of basic literacy and is as much, and will be much, more of a literacy index as any other.

We, in CMC, have been looking at computers and the applicability in bringing about improvement in the quality of life. In fact, we have been looking at 'information technology' (IT) for improvement in the quality of life which involves more than what is meant by the word "computers". IT incorporates communication and other forms of electronic media, storage eta., in addition to computers. Our effort has been to deploy this technology to bring about a perceptible change in the quality of life including social and economic dimensions; aspects of education and training; aspects of social welfare; health and such other areas. Here, however, we would like to focus on education and training using computers which has essentially

*By P.P. Gupta.

two facets—one being education about computers and the other being education through computers. In both these aspects, that we will look at, CMC has had extensive experience. As a national organisation in the field of information technology, CMC reorganised the need for computer education, computer awareness and computer literacy in this country as early as in 1978-79 and started a programme which has progressively increased in quality and value. Today we are in the neighbourhood of 300 short and long programmes every year which just about cover all parts of the country. CMC's education and training programme has involved almost 30,000 manweeks of training imparted and a participant range of over 12,000. We have, thus, eight years of experience in such learning with a range of people. People who are new to computers; people who are veterans in management and went to pursue understanding of machines; people who are computer scientists and wish to know what is going on in the field of computers elsewhere in the world. Thus we find ourselves in a very unique position to comment on the kind of education and training programmes that computers need to be used for, and on the kind of training that can be imparted in the field of computers. The other aspect that we would like to address is the fact that computers can become an extremely useful mode of transferring knowledge. A lot has already been stated on this subject and it is not my intention to turn this into a very technical presentation on Computer Aided Learning. What I would like to briefly cover is, what CMC is doing and what our experience has been in very general terms and where we need to put our priorities with regard to the use of computers for learning. The training through the use of computers could be in any field of activity. However, education and training in the field of information technology has a very special significance for the simple reason that technology is changing extremely fast. Also, with the change of technology there is a change in techno-economic and social aspects all of which require rethinking, reassessment and concept evaluation of a lot of management aspects that go hand in hand with the application of such technology. Anybody in the fied of information technology actually goes through a process of constant learning, just like other areas of fast changing technologies such as medicine. The first salient aspect of this approach is that there is substantial intra profession learning, that is one has to continuously learn from others in the profession.

Secondly, experience is not necessarily a substitute a or replacement for knowledge. Quite often we see advertisements which require either a particular qualification or so many years of experience. Such requirements are no longer valid.

Thirdly, one has to learn from a lot of people who are younger or less experienced and one faces serious competition in the profession from people who are significantly younger unless one keeps oneself abreast with latest developments. The younger people have substantial advantage in terms of their preparedness for the adaptation of rapidly advancing technology and its implementation.

An essential aspect of technology development in the field of information technology has been a very fast transition from the stage of research and development into a stage of technology implementation bringing about concrete economic benefit. In other words from a stage of technological advances to products and processes which actually deliver the goods in a more cost-effective and efficient manner.

A commensurate infrastructure is required to take advantage of economic benefits in the rapid process so that when the next wave of technology development and new versions of products and processes become available, certain amount of benefit has been derived from the previous cycle. This sharp reduction in the total period available for economic exploitation makes it absolutely necessary for the society, the beneficiary, to not only learn how to use the technology but also learn to use it in all best possible ways.

The requirement thus is to be able to rapidly adapt oneself to the new technology, take full advantage of it, unlearn and keep repeating this cycle ever so often. In other words, the validity of knowledge once a new technology comes through is for a very short period, that is, until the next wave of technology comes. The validity period is, moreover, increasingly becoming shorter. This process of learning, applying, unlearning and learning again has interesting implications with respect to learning strategies.

First of all, effective methods of dissemination of information have to be developed, so that during the short period available utilisation of technology is maximised.

Secondly, more effective learning processes are required in order to quickly grasp and apply new concepts.

Thirdly, a large amount of flexibility in attitudes is necessary in order to get adjusted to the process of unlearning and relearning, whatever the age of the person.

We now come to the role and significance of computers in this dynamic environment of fast changing technologies resulting in shrinking cycles of learning, applying and unlearning. Also how computers can become inherent in any strategy formulation in this kind of environment.

As we all know computers have the potential of helping in the process of learning in many ways. As we look at the strategies of learning in general, we have the phase of knowledge absorption, which in the first cognitive input from the teacher to the student. The next stage is that of using this knowledge to practise through a drill, the implementation of this knowledge. It is here that we can identify the weakness of the student and reinforce learning. The reinforcement must be effected through drill and practice. We also have the aspect of testing which requires evaluation and record keeping. And last but not the least we must have some tools to enhance the process of effective learning. These would include the devices of demonstration, models and simulation.

The primary question with regard to the use of computers for learning, is whether computers would be used as a replacement for teachers. In other words whether the computer will actually perform all tasks that teachers are expected to perform and whether it is possible to achieve a 'human' relationship between the computer and pupil. The answer is obviously no. The teacher actually uses computers as an aid. A certain amount of computer time is made available to a student so that the student is able to reinforce the input which he has received from the teacher. It has been observed that where the computer is used as an aid to learning it is more effective than the complete replacement of a teacher by a computer or a computer terminal. However, there is some merit of using the complete replacement approach in certain areas where it has been tried and has been found quite successful. I think we could take a lesson from some of the situations in other parts of the world. Such complete replacement situations have arisen in the state of Alaska, for example, where there are very far flung and remote areas where teachers are just not available. Where communities actually live and children have to be taught. Or in the parts of Australia where they started with wireless education and now have gone on to Computer Aided Instruction.

A related issue is that of lack of availability of competent and effective teachers which is very much a reality in our country. I think in a situation like this, if we look at information technology including facilities such as communications, satellite technology, computers and TV broadcasting, we can think of some very exciting applications in the field of learning. Of the experiments that have been conducted in the country one of the most interesting is CLASS (Computer Literacy and Studies in Schools). Another experiment is the satellite education programme that has been initiated by the Ministry of Education. One can foresee a combination of the two emerging on the Indian scene with immense implications in terms of learning processes and modalities. A combination of broadcasting as well as Computer Aided Education has paid rich dividends in many parts of the world. In UK, for example,

Computer Aided instruction software is actually broadcast over networks of computers from a central point where it is created. The distribution to a large number of institutions all over the country is done through standard communication lines. All subscribers to this activity are entitled to receive and keep copies of the software for their use.

We now come to some more specific issues relating to automation in learning. If we look at some of the positive sides of computers as an aid to learning, the possibilities are very exciting. For one thing, there is no other method which complements the teacher more effectively simply because computers are interactive. In other words a student and the computer have a sort of conversation in much the same way that two people converse with each other and in this process learning or exchange of information is meaningful and effective.

Using computers, the coverage in terms of students, is very large. With a well prepared lesson any number of copies can be made with relative ease at very low cost and therefore the number of students who can be benefitted by it is only limited by the number of machines one can make available.

The next important aspect is that automated learning of this kind is very convenient in the light of the differences in students. Students could be very intelligent, less intelligent or handicapped for several reasons. Due to differences of background and intelligence, different students have varied speeds of learning. A method of learning which is self-paced is, therefore, as effective as a teacher teaching one student at a time. Computer Aided Learning has the potential of being self-placed to the extent of treating every individual as an individual.

A teacher is now relieved of the burden of a lot of routine teaching, which requires more presentation in a fairly mechanical sort of way. This allows him more time and attention to creative tasks of devising interesting and new methods of teaching. New models, new ideas, new strategies of teaching can be captured and delivered by the computer while the teacher is engaged in making learning more effective.

One can not delay the fact that a very good teacher often does not want to teach the same topic repetitively. It is a case of simple boredom. Cognitive input variations, in terms of quality, responsiveness to students and overall effectiveness get taken care of extremely competently by the computerised aids in learning,

Frequently, a teacher is not in a mental frame to perform at his best. As a consequence it is the poor student who suffers. A lot of these aspects can be eliminated by catching the teachers in their best possible mood to capture his teaching skills effectively and then deliver it as many times as required, with out burdening the teachers. I think one of the most significant aspects of Computer Aided Learning is the fact that one can use the computer in a completely novel sort of way and use teaching methods which are simply impossible otherwise. These are possibilities of a whole range of demonstrations and simulations which computers have made possible through the process of animation, simulation; interesting graphics with movement; interesting sound graphics and colours with modelling and communication. All of these can be integrated into the learning process to enable the student to learn as effectively as possible and to enable the teacher to devise the best possible teaching method for the specific subject to be learnt.

Another important capability of the computer is to take away a lot of administrative burden from the teacher. The computer can maintain records, conduct tests, prepare question papers and go through a process of grading which can be fairly mechanical at times for the teacher.

Having looked at the advantages of computer aided learning, I think it is wise to look at some of the possible weaknesses which we should be aware of before we plunge head long into Computer Aided Learning and its applications.

It is very important to recognise the fact that there is a possibility of a process of dehumanization taking place in this whole effort which must be avoided. There is really no substitute for a good teacher, that, I think, is a widely accepted fact.

There is a need for systems which capture the intelligence of a teacher and make the interface between the computer programme which teaches and the student, as intelligent as possible. It is in recognition of this need that substantial research is being undertaken the world over. Until that is achieved, Computer Aided Learning will remain a bit of a challenge for researchers.

The Indian context paints a fascinating and compelling picture. We have had the opportunity of working with the CLASS project which I have mentioned earlier. The CLASS project allows any organisation to contribute to this pool of education software a course of module for the schools. Once it is approved and accepted, the course will be distributed to all the installations of CLASS all over the country. Computers available to these schools are being used by the teacher as a tool, since a situation where one student alone is facing a computer for any significant length of time to learn from the computer by himself is not possible at this juncture. We have, therefore, looked at the programme as one which is used by the teacher to demonstrate some of the concepts which are otherwise either extremely difficult or completely impossible to demonstrate. Some of these programmes have been developed by CMC and now are being distributed among schools which are within the CLASS project. These have proved effective for students to learn concepts which are very difficult to teach without the aid of very expensive equipment which is not available in most schools. With computers, images can be made to move and it is possible to display structures like molecular formation and change. So music or sound, a picture, colour and movement have created a new context of learning.

In summation I would like to emphasize two fundamental aspects of this relationship between learning and information technology. Firstly, information technology more than any other involves a rapidly reducing cycle of learning, applying, unlearning, relearning and applying. This is the most poignant remainder underlining the concept of continuous learning in every day life. This also implies that knowledge as valid today would stand out dated and obsolete in a very short time, and that new strategies to cope with the anxieties of differential learning in terms of age and other attributes of the learner must emerge.

Secondly, Computer Aided Learning from its nascence as a "Teachine Machine" of the 60's has reaehed the threshold of its adolescence, where immense possibilities that combine artificial intelligence, communications and Computer Aided Learning into an almost entirely new context of learning, are a reality today.

Therefore, computers in learning are perhaps strategically the most crucial facet that demand a re-examination of existing approaches to learning itself.

II

INFORMATION STORAGE AND RETRIEVAL SYSTEMS*

A good records management system is the one that helps an organisation to store, preserve and retrieve promptly the documents and information actually needed by the management and employees.

The basic objectives of such a system are those of use (present and future), protection (chiefly legal), and reduction in costs. The factors of use and costs greatly outweigh the consi-

*By R.S. Rathore.

deration of protection for the great majority of records. Legal requirements would justify storage of only an extremely small portion of records.

Most records control programmes, therefore, seek to aim at a system which would provide the case or facility of prompt storage and retrieval of records at minimum costs both in terms of human effort and money. They also aim at capturing data at the point of creation for reasons of reliability and accuracy.

Where storage and retrieval functions are mechanised, storage of information and data is usually handled in one or several of the following ways:

Edge-Match cards

Scan-Match cards

Optical coincidence

Microfilming

Punched cards

Paper Tape

Computer-systems

The card systems for storage and retrieval of information and data have been in use for many years. However, in today's world of automation these relatively simple systems are often overlooked. This class of systems has several outstanding features, such as being close to the user. For small jobs, these are effective and in my view these must at least be considered when designing a system.

Edge Notched Cards

In this system, the cards, which could vary in size and shape but each serving a particular application, are coded by notches or holes along the edges of the card.

These notches or holes are made with the assistance of prepunched pilot holes. The notching allows selective sorting. By making several "passes" with a needle which is done by putting a needle through the appropriate pilot hole portion in a deck or cards and lifting the needle to all the notched cards to fall—the cards that meet the search are selected.

Special hand punches for single row notching, for joining two holes to form a lot, or for U notching double row coding, and Keysort sorting needle are available. The sorting needle is a steel needle set in a plastic handle. An alignment block for increasing the speed and ease of sorting is also sometime used. The advantages of this system include low costs, and the closeness to the user. Its disadvantages are:

(a) only a few cards can be searched with one pass of the needle, and
(b) the size of the sorting 'vocabulary' is limited to the size of the card.

Scan Column Card System

In this system, instead of having one card per document item (as is the case with Edge-notched cards system) there is one card per descriptive term. The items are given accession number which are posted on the cards (by hand or typewritten) in the appropriate column according to the right hand digit. All accession numbers, for example, ending with a 2 (*i.e.* 12, 32, 102, 5042, etc.) are placed in descending order in the column headed by "2" as under.

The cards are alphabetically arranged. When new items are to be added, the appropriate cards are taken out and accession numbers written or typed under the right column heading. Then the cards are refiled.

For a search, the appropriate search cards are selected and the accession numbers compared column by column. For better see also—

see—

TERM: Radios

0	1	2	3	4	5
		2	33		65
		12	63		85
		32			

(To search, the Accssion Numbers, are Matched with those of another Pertinent card.)

speed, the comparison is done with the least amount of accession numbers.

The advantages of this system are:

1. inexpensive,
2. new terms can be added by adding new cards,
3. conversion to computer system is relatively easy.

Its disadvantages are:

1. the store of items is separate from the retrieval function and requires a separate look up
2. the search can become cumbersome if the size of the system is very large.

Optical Coincidence

In this system, one card is assigned per one descriptive characteristic, and the accession number tie the store to the optical concidence device. The accession number are not printed or typed on a card but the number is drilled into a unique x-y co-ordination position. This is done by selecting the termwise cards and one set at a time is placed into an input drilling device. These—upto 30 or 50—are all put into the machine at one time. The drill is positioned in the appropriate x-y position, denoting the required accession number, and then holes are simultaneously made through all of the cards.

To retrieve information, pertinent term cards are selected and superimposed in a reader. A conjunctive search (term A, term B, term C, etc.) is done very rapidly (about 10,000 items in a minute). The cards have a 100×100 matrix; thus each set of characteristic cards have a capacity of 10,000 items.

Its advantages include rapid search, relatively rapid input and few limitations on vocabulary. Its disadvantages inculde constant checking of inputs and cost.

Microfilm

Microfilm technique for storage of records is not new. In fact, there is evidence to show that the first microphotographic technique was used as early as in 1839.

In recent years, however, the development and perfection of microfilming technique has greatly alerted "the dual process of placing records in storage and retrieving information from stores records." This technique has been found very useful in solving the growing storage problem that exists in almost every organisation.

In this process, the equipment required consists of a camera (available for film sizes 8mm, 16mm, 70mm, and 105mm), a film reader for projecting images, photoprinting attachments, and cabinets for storing films. The cameras and readers are available with a wide range of capacities and special features. These featnres give the following facilities:

(a) Photocopy can be obtained;

(b) Width of film used could be flexible;

(c) Permits records to be reduced in size to save space;

(d) Choice of size;

(e) Clearer image;

(f) Retrieval of a particular record made easier by placing short black marks between frames or computers;

(g) High capacity portable units combining all functions are also available.

The storage of records is done by photographing at high speed on narrow safety film which are then developed to create the masterform. The film can be retained indefinitely. From the master, duplicate copies can normally be prepared. Letters and legal sized papers are usually filmed on 8mm or 16mm but engineering drawings, maps, etc. are filmed on 35mm or 70mm. The popular size are 16mm and 35mm. The process of retrieval is accomplished by placing the film on a reader and locating the record by the use of microfilm code system. A photocopy of the record can be obtained if required.

The records may be mircrofilmed in the following formats:

Roll Film: Documents are filmed sequentially on to a roll of film 16mm/35mm wide and 100ft. long. One film can contain upto 5000 images or papers.

Microfiche: On a single sheet of film, (3×5 inch, 4×6 inch or 5×8 inch size), some 98 to 100 images are exposed. concept is the same—put a document on a single piece of film, then it can be disseminated interfiled, and stored as required. Unlike roll film, unrelated documents need not have to do along with pertinent ones. Many copies of each microfiche can be made for dissemination.

Cartridge/Magazines: This enables automatic threading and loading of various elements of microfilm. It is like cassette tape. Just turn a switch, the film is automatically threaded.

Jackets: The jacket approach gives the function of the microfiche while allowing film images to be added as required. The jacket is a series of pokets were frames or series of frames taken on a roll of film are cut and placed in jackets or sleeves.

Aperture Card: A simple 35mm frame is mounted on a punched card to create an Aperture Card. This is widely used for engineering designs or maps. We can punch code numbers on the card and use unit record equipment to sort or manipulate records.

Ultrafiche: Usually reduction ratio in roll films is 20 to 1. In this process, it can be as much as 150 to 1. In this approach, we can put upto 3200 pages on a 4×6 inch sheet of film, and these can be duplicated at a very small cost.

Microfilm process for storage of records is now very popular in developed countries though it is not yet widely used in India. This is because most organisations are now faced with mass storage problems. Mass production of the microfilming equipment has also brought down their prices.

Its greatest advantage is space saving. On a 100 fit. roll, we can store as many as 5000 letters of standard size and in 3 fit. high cabinet we can store 600 rolls. This process also provides legal protection as filmed records are now admissible in most law courts and above all it ensures records preservation and safety. The passage of time causes less deterioration of film than would occur with original paper documents. Hand copies of important documents can be stored separately.

The facilities of rapid look-up of large number of records in a few seconds, rapid exact printing, and easy and low cost mailing make microfilm a very useful and important means of storage of records. Its potentialities are almost unlimited. Now the microfilms are being used as a means of computer output. Systems are currently available which take information stored on magnetic tapes, convert it into images on a T.V. screen (called cathode ray tubes) and photograph these images on microfilm. Its cost, at least in India, is still a prohibiting factor.

The system consideration for their use should include:

1. Is the collection growing?
2. Is the information used frequently?
3. The legal implications—some documents have to be preserved for a certain number of years.

It is essential that the system should be made simple for use.

Punched Cards

One of the most commonly used media for storage is a Punched Card. These cards have been in use ever since Dr. Herman Hollerith adopted these in 1887 for U.S. Census. Basically, the punched card is a piece of high quality paper of a uniform and precise thickness cut to exact measurements. The dimensions of the card on all three planes—length, breadth and thickness—must be uniform and precise for being used as satisfactory medium for feeding data into the computer.

There are a number of varieties of punched cards—of 40 column, 65 column, 80 column, 90 column, 120 column, etc. The most widely used is the 80 column card which uses the Hollerith punched card coding system. The size of an 80 column card is 7.3/8 inch long and 3.1/4 inch wide.

Information is recorded on punched cards by means of holes punched in specified positions known as columns. In the case of 80 column cards using Hollerith coding system, the holes are rectangular in shape while in the power system these are round holes. In Hollerith coding system, the card is divided into 80 vertical columns. There are 12 possible points in a vertical column of the card on which holes can be punched; these are called the Punching Positions. Both the number of column and punching positions (0 to 9 only) are printed on the cards for facility of punching, but this is not absolutely essential.

How are data represented on the cards? The data are recorded on the cards by punching holes. Each column of the card is able to accommodate a digit, an alphabet or a special character like £,$,%, etc. In a 90 column card we can thus have a maximum of 80 individual characters.

12, 11 and O punching positions (also sometimes called A and B positions) are not printed but the top edge of the card is punching position "12" (also known as 12 edge) and the 11th position is between 'O' and '12' punching positions. The bottom edge of the card is known as "9" edge.

One, two or three holes can be punched in any column to represent a numeric digit, alphabetical letter or a special character like £, Rs. $, @ etc. The numeric digit is recorded by punching a single punch in the row associated with that digit. Thus to record digit 8, only a single punch in any column in the row '8' is necessary.

12, 11 and O punching positions are called "zone punches". A combination of a zone punch position and numeric punch position is used to represent alphabet, A to I, are coded by combination of a punch in the 12 punch position and the numeric punches 1 to 9. Letters J to R are coded by an 11 punch and digits 1 to 9. S to Z, the last 8 letters, are the combination of the 0 Zone punch and digits 2 to 9. Eleven special characters are recorded by one, two or three punches. Their function is to provide printed symbols as required, to cause certain machinery operations to occur, or to identify specific cards. "It is important to relise that the literal meaning of any hole or combination of holes is not necessarily the only meaning. The punched holes can be given virtually any significance."

Cards are divided into segments called "fields". A field is a column or a group of columns reserved for the punching of specific data. The field may be numerical, alphabetical or alphanumeric and its length depends upon the requirements. For example, a 'data' field may be 6 column large—2 for date, 1 for month and 2 for year, while a name field may be as large as 20-25 column. Machine processing requires (though not always essential) a standard arrangement of data in the card. Field assignment and card layout are usually made after analysis of individual needs.

Cards may be punched by Hand punch, Automatic Key punch machine, or by a Mark sensing key punch machine (not yet available in India) or produced even as an output by the computer itself for any subsequent input. The key punch machines have a keyboard similar to a typewriter. The operator has to depress a key to punch combination of holes required to represent a particular character. As the key is depressed, the numbers of holes required to represent the character are automatically punched in a column. In hand punches, however, the number of holes required will have to be punched separately. In some key punch machines the character punched in each column is also typed on the top edge of each column which makes it easier to verify what has been punched. Key punch machines are produced in India.

Cards can also be punched under the direction of the computer through a device known as Card punch but this is done only when output is required in the form of a punched card perhaps for subsequent input The card punch machine has a punching speed of 250 cards to 500 cards per minute.

Devices for reading the contents of punched cards into the computers vary considerably in external appearance and in the purely mechanical method of moving successive cards past the "reading station". The essential factor is the speed at which cards may be read. Card readers for computers vary in speed ranging between 600 cards to 1500 cards a minute or more. Majority of them have a speed ranging between 600 to 900.

The cards are read by the card readers either by using a brush or photo-electric sensing. In the brush type reader, the cards move under a set of reading brushes. These brushes, sense the presence or absence of holes in the card and convert the data into electrical impulses. In some card readers, a second set of brushes reads the card again as a check.

In a photo-electric reader, the card passes over a light souree and the presence or absence of the holes is noted by photo-electric cells. Except for this technique of reading there is little difference between the two types of card readers. Their function of detecting data and converting them into electrical impulses is the same.

Punched cards are widely used because these are one of the cheapest media of transferring data into the computer. Among their many advantages are ease of programming, ease of correction in case of wrong punching of holes, ease of sorting, ease of storing and capability for semi-permanent storage. These can be prepunched and used for such applications as insurance premia notices; eleetricity bills where these can later be used as input. Thus in an insurance premia application, the policy number, the premium amount and the month/quarter to which it relates may be prepunched and sent to the insured who returns this card along with his cheque. This card is then used to update his policy record by recording that the particular premium has been paid. However, in many places, these are being gradually discarded and replaced by other media. This is because the punched cards have the limitation of mechanical handling causing low speed; low capacity to hold data (only 80 characters on a card), These are also more prone to errors; occupy lot of storage space; sensitive to humidity and are uneconomical on account of expenditure on labour costs in punching and verifying.

Paper Tape

Paper tape is another means of getting information into the computer. Punched paper tape consists of a continuous strip of paper tape in which data are recorded serially by punching holes across the tape. The tape, which can be one of the two standard widths, 11/16 inch and 1 inch, need not necessarily be made of paper, it is also obtainable in a tape made of thin flexible plastic compounds.

Data are recorded on paper tape by punching holes across the tape. The characters an the tape are each recorded as a row of holes across the tape, each character being represented by a unique combination of holes. The width of the tape is divided into seven or eight tracks in 1" wide and 5 or 6 tracks in 11/16 inch wide tape. The tape width is divided into two portions by a hole in the middle known as "sprocket hole" which is used for moving the paper tape.

The paper tape can be created in several ways:

By key-operated paper tape punches (like card punches);

By conversion from punched card on an automatic card controlled tape punch;

As a result of the operation of a teleprinter;

As the output from the computer itself.

The reading device for paper tape is known as Paper Tape Reader which is very similar in operation to card readers.

One advantage of paper tape is that the data it contains can be in variable length (as against fixed length of 80 columns in punched cards) since it is a continuous strip or roll. Another advantage is that while cards must be read (or punched) one at a time, paper tape can be read continuously. Less time (as compared to cards) is lost in reading by Paper Tape devices because of the continuity of the medium. Paper tape usually means faster transfer of data into or out of comptuer. A great advantage of paper tape is that it can be prepared as a by-product of the several kinds of other office machines like type-writers and teleprinters.

But paper tape is not perfect. It is not as durable as punched cards, nor is it convenient to handle. And data cannot be rearranged or manipulated as in cards where each card is a unit.

Punched cards should not be used where some sort of semi-permanent storage is required, or inputs have to be resorted, where punching errors are high (because punched cards can be corrected) and some record keeping is required. Paper tapes could be used where data after punching have to be sent to remote locations, and where data can be obtained on teleprinter lines, and where pre-sorting of records is to be done on a mechanical sorter. Paper tape is cheaper and records cannot go out of sequence; it is less bulky, hence easier to transmit to remote locations, and is easier to feed to computer than cards. It is also compatible with telex machines.

Magnetic Tape

One of the most commonly used external storage medium is Magnetic Tape. Much faster than punched cards and paper tape, it is used as an input medium, as an output medium, and also as an external storage medium where its main function is to store information to be processed later by the computer.

Most of us are familiar with home tape recorders. The magnetic tape used in computer systems is very similar in appearance to the used in tape recorders except that the width of computer magnetic tapes is different. It varies from $\frac{1}{2}$ inch (.51″ to be precise) to one inch and one reel of tape is approximately

2400 feet in length, although magnetic tape is available in lengths of 1200 feet to 3000 feet per reel. The most popular lengths are 1200 and 2400 feet. The Honey weel 400 computers available with Government of India use ¾ inch wide tapes while IBM computers use ½inch tapes.

The concept of recording information on megnetic medium dates back to 1880's when efforts were made to use a wire to store electrical signals. Later on, a German company succeeded in producing a magnetic film coated tape. These principles were 'copied and improved' subsequently and today magnetic tapes are used in a wide a variety of tape recorders, business machines, dictaphones, television programmes (video tapes), and in automatic control of industrial processes.

A magnetic tape used in computers consist of a strip of thin plastic base material (usually polyester plastic) with a coating of ferro-magnetic on one side only. The coating is held to a tolerance of+ 0.000012 inch to assure proper performance. This coating makes the tapes capable of receiving magnetised spots of either of two polarities 0 and 1. The device upon which the magnetic tape reels are mounted is known as Magnetic Tape unit. A tape unit or deck has two reel holders, a supply reel holder and a takeup reel holder. In addition, it has a tape drive mechanism for moving the tape, and a read-write head (like recording head in a tape recorder) for reading from and writing or recording on the tape. There is also a tape reservoir, a vacuum chamber for ensuring even movement of tape.

Data are read from or are written on to magnetic tape according to computer commands. The tape drive mechanism moves the tape past a read-write head. The tape reel is first loaded on to the supply reel holder and threaded around a number of rollers which physically moves the tape from the supply reel holder to the take-up. In some modern tape units, the threading is automatically done.

Data are read from the tape as magnetised spots pass the readhead, generating thereby electrical impulses. These impulses represent the data in an electronic form. The circuitry of the tape drive then makes these electronic data available to computer.

Like home tape recorders, reading from tape (like playing the tape) is non-destructive that is to say the data recorded on tape can be retained on it for indefinite period and it can be retrieved as many times as required without the fear of losing it. However, writing on the tape is destructtve, that is whatever is already recorded is erased and the new data overlay the earlier data which are destroyed, Actually this is done by a proceess of overlaying and is similar to the home tape recorders. Electrical impulses from the computer (*i.e.* data) are deposited as magnetic spots along the tape. These spots are called 'bits' (binary digit) and are arranged in a specific order to signify numbers, alphabets and special characters.

The number of bits that can be recorded on an inch of tape is called Packing Density. Packing Density is defined as "The greatest possible number of columns of data can be recorded on a unit length of tape." The unit used is usually an inch. Depending upon the type of magnetic tape unit used, this density can be anywhere between 100 bpi (bits per inch) and 2400 bpi or even more in some modern tape units. This means that the contents of as many as 10 punched cards can be stored in one inch length of tape, with a packing density of 800 bpi. On one reel of tape millions of characters can be stored, almost as much as can be stored on 2 to 3 lakh punch cards.

Writing on tapes can be done at a density of 800 bpi or greater. The transfer rate *i.e.* rate at which data can be read from or written on to a tape could be anywhere from 20,000 characters or 20 kch (k=1000, ch=character) to 96,000 characters (96 kch) per second. This is tremendous when we recall that a card reader can read only 48000 characters per minute or 800 characters per second, a a paper tape reader can read only 1000 characters per second. and the card punch can punch only 133 characters per second and a paper tape can punch only 100 characters per second.

Why Use Tapes?

The magnetic tape has become popular both as an input and output medium and external storage medium because of its speed of access (a wholé reel of tape can be read in 4 to 12 minutes), its capacity for storing data (several million characters), its subsequent re-use, its cheapness (a tape reel is cheaper in terms of equivalent number of cards required), permanence and flexibility. Tape can be read much faster than punched cards or paper tape. As a compact method of storing and handling data it has attracted most computer users. What can be stored in one reel of tape requiring a few hundred squares of inch will require approximately 100 square feet of space to store cards containing as much data. Its flexibility is evidenced by the fact that records can be of variable length.

Its disadvantages include the fact that data must be read or written sequentially, and a lot must be moved to find a particular record, just as in the case of tape recorders. Therefore, they are not popular for jobs or applications which require quick searching for specific data. Thus where response time for retrieving data is to be few seconds as in the case of criminal records or airline reservation, tapes are not used.

Disc

Magnetic disc storage devices have relatively shorter access time and large storage capacity. The disc unit is a stack of flat, round rotating discs resembling gramophone records. A disc storage device usually comprises a cartridge of six discs which are permanently fixed to the device. Each disc has two recording surfaces (one on each of the two sides) with ten read/write heads attached to a movable arm (like the gramophone needle) positioned over the disc. These heads permit the writing on or reading from a disc as it rotates. The data are stored in the standard code of magnetised spots in concentric circles on the coated surfaces of the discs.

Storage locations on the disc can be referred to or assigned by the computer—locations are determined on certain levels of storage, zone track, sector, etc. Data can be read from or written on any section of any disc. Therefore, data can be stored on discs in random order. When the computer wants to refer to a piece of data, it goes directly to the correct spot on the disc. It does not have to serially search for the data as it does in the case of tapes. Discs are also known as Random Access Device. They can also be used as Input-Output devices.

As is magnetic tapes, reading from discs is not destructive but writing is. A record is written on the disc by a process of overlay simiar to that on tapes. Reading and writing is accomplished through the read-write heads located on each surface but all the ten read-write heads move in unison. When in operation, the complete cartridge of six discs rotates and therefore on each of the ten surfoces of the six discs each part of the track at which the head assembly is currently positioned passes in turn by its associated read-write head.

Discs have a large storage capacity for storing data. Depending upon the model, one disc cartridge of ten surfaces can store as much as 4 to 10 million characters (in some recent models even more). This is no doubt less than what can be stored on a magnetic tape but the access time on discs is far less than the tapes. The average access time is about 25—75 millisecs. Each record can be accessed directly unlike in tape where rcords have to be accessed sequentially. It is for this reason that discs are known as Direct Access Storage Devices or Random Access Devices. As many as 9 disc packs can be hooked to a system providing a very large storage capacity.

Direct Access Devices like discs are costlier than a magnetic tape but what makes them more acceptable is their fast access time and greater on-line capacity, *i.e.* they provide immediate response time. For storing and compiling, they are about ten times faster than magnetic tapes. The criteria for choosing discs are mainly the volume, cost and time. Usually they are preferred to tapes when fast response time is required as in airlines reservations or criminal records search, when all records are not to be serially accessed, *i.e.*, when activity is low. Thus they are used for storing programmes, tables for scientific work, and for keeping such data as are required to be accessed promptly.

Drum

A Magnetic Drum is another form of storage device. A magnetic drum is a cylinder coated with a special alloy. This coating on the surface of the drum is the medium on which the bits of data are recorded and stored. The drum rotates, or rather spins, at a constant speed beneath combined read-write heads, one head for each track or circular section of the drum. These heads read and write data in almost the same manner as those on the tape unit. The drum is divided into individual sections, each having an addrese and each capable of storing a number of characters of data. These locations can be assigned, allocated and referred to by the computer. Reading and writing of data can only occur when the specific locations of the data involved pass under the read-write heads. So access time will depend upon the distance the drum has to travel to bring that location under the head. However, some magnetic drums have special, fast access areas with four read-writ heads on each track. This way, only a quarter-turn instead of a full revolution of the drum is the maximum delay in reading information stored at a specific location. The storage capacity of drums ranges from 1million to 3.91 million characters per drum. Average access time ranges from 2.5 to 5 millisecs.

Both discs and drums are storage devices, *i.e.* you may go directly to any spot on the drum and use the information found there. In this, they have an advantage over tape where sequential access only is possible. The capacity of drum storage is relatively smaller but, faster than Disc where access time is slow, but storage capacity is higher. Both discs and drums are more expensive than tapes though their cost is largely offset by their ability to provide competers with prompt and direct access to millons of specific storage locations.

Data Cell

In the data cells, the information is stored on a strip of magnetic tape. This tape is wide enough to accept 100 tracks of data. The method of storage is similar to the magnetic tapes. The strips are made of tapo with a magnetic oxide coating on one side. Each strip is 2½″ wide, 13″ long and about three times as thick as magnetic tape. The strips are held in place by the bottom of the cell and by the adjacent strips. When the computer needs access to information in the data cell, this strip is actually taken out of the data cell, wrapped around a drum and then read with twenty read-write heads of the data cell drive unit, and then placed back after having been read or written on. The cell when removed from the drive is encosed in protective covers. All this is mechanically done under the command of the computer. A strip has a maximum capacity of 400 million characters. The access time is however slow ranging from 175 to 600 milliseconds depending upon the model.

The data cell drives are slow because a lot of mechanical movement is involved. However, since each data cell is removable, it allows virtually unlimited storage capacity.

The comparative figures of access time and storage capacity for some of the models of discs, drums, and data cells are—

	Access Time	*Storage Capacity*
Disc	25 to 135 millisecs (av. 75 millisecs)	10 million characters
Drum	8.6 millisecs	3.91 million characters
Data Cell	175 to 600 millisecs	400 million characters

The advantages of Direct Access Storage Devices are:

Any record can be accessed without extensive search of other records (not possible in tapes).

Transactions can be processed on-line.

More than one file can be stored on the same device and accesssed during the same job. In tapes, we will have to keen them on separate tape units.

They eliminate or at least reduce the time for presorting the input data.

CONSIDERATIONS FOR SELECTING A MEDIA

It is difficult to lay down a rule of thumb for selecting a particular medium of storage and retrieval of information for any organisation. The potentials of edgenotched cards, scan-match cards or optical coincidence are essentially limited. Mierofilming is an excellent medium of storage and retrieval but in India its costs may be a maior limiting factor. The other storage media discussed above fall in the realm of computer systems, although punched cards and paper tape can be used even in a non-computer environment. There is an advantage in using them even in a small organisation because it would be easier then to subsequently switch on to a computer system or to a Untt-Record System. It is, however, possible to say how one could discover potential areas for use of data processing techniques forstorage and retrieval of information. There are five major clues—Repetition, Volume, Speed, Errors, and Complexity: the first two clues will always be present in a potential application at least in non-scientific areas of application while the other clues if found, would add to the justification for use of data processing equipment.

Repetition—By this we do not imply repetitive tasks but repetition of data. The use of repetitive data over and over again on the same form in a paper work system is what we should look for. Each time the form is used it may contain different data from the previous time but an analysis of the many forms used during a period of time might show the same data appearing from time to time or at regular intervals. A good example will be preparation of an invoice. The customer's name and address may remain the same even though we do not sell him same thing everytime.

Volume does not imply total work load but volume of repetitive data. Repetition of data is the key to our potential data processing application and volume of repetitive data may be the principal justification. An example may be 2 lakh invoices every month of year. What we should be looking for is the number of times that repetitive data are used in a complete paperwork cycle. Categories of volume include gross volume (like number of invoices or employees for a payroll application) and dispersed volume (like reporting of census figures or tax collected industrywise).

Urgency implies the requirement of speed. Use of computers may help meet realistic deadlines. This can be particulary useful where peak loads are involved. For example, project progress reports are received frequently in a central office reflecting conditions at the close of the month. These statistics must be compiled and put up to management by the fifth of the succeeding month if the report is to be timely and useful to management. This kind of operation has the repetitive data, repetitive volume and urgency we are seeking. Urgency alone could be sufficient justification but it is often the 'boil' that causes us to look at the paper work cycle and to find the repetitive volume data that is involved. In some areas such as Air Defence Systems, the requirement of speed of response time may be very critical.

Errors are not usually sufficient reasons for introducing data processing unless they involve repetitive data. We should look for the human errors in the volume of repetitive data—human errors of transcription, transportation or mathematical computation. These are errors that a machine properly operated will not make. Many of these errors could perhaps be avoided by capturing data at the point of creation itself.

Complexity is usually not associated with commercial applications but there are certain areas of work which are so complex and require such extra ordinary speed that they cannot be done without the use of computers. Examples of these would be crime records, criminal identification, traffic planning and control, forecasting and projections in financial or sales or production estimates. This consideration of complexity and requirements of speed is most often found in scientific application like space flights. This would also be found in Early Warning Air Defence Systems.

Where to look for? Potential areas of computerisation can "turn up" anywhere. Usually these would be found at points where information is recorded about persons, places, things, or where more than one form is used in a paperwork system, or where statistical reports originate.

Conclusion

Finally, a word of caution. We can setect any medium for storage of information but in doing so, we must take a systems approach. This implies a carefully done feasibility or systems study which should be followed by constant monitoring and evaluation of the system so that the system 'lives' and not merely exists. We must remember that many good systems have become obsolete or even proved a nightmare when not maintained or when not constantly serviced. How this should be ensured is however a different subject altogether.

10

Information and its Flow in an Organisation: Case of ONGC

H. KUMAR

This article begins with a general statement on the importance of adequate information in different areas for the effective management of any organization, particularly a large one. The Oil and Natural Gas Commission (ONGC), one of India's biggest and most dynamic corporations, is then taken as an example and a study is made of the information systems in use. Certain weaknesses are pointed out and a suggestion made that only a well programmed, completely integrated, fully computerized information system can satisfy the growing needs the Commission.

What is Information?

"Information is defined as some tangible or intangible entity which serves to reduce uncertainty about some future state or event." As an example, consider a weather forecast predicting clear and sunny weather tomorrow; this information reduces our uncertainty whether an event such as a cricket match will be held. Information that a bank has just made a firm a loan, reduces uncertainty whether it shall be solvent or bankrupt next month. Another definition of information has been suggested by Davis (1974):

> "Information is data that has been processed into a form that is meaningful to the recipient and of real perceived value in current or perspective decisions[2]." This definition of information stresses the fact that data have to be processed in some way to produce information: information is more than raw data.

It is apparent that within any organisation the totality of its information may be subdivided into a number of groups. Below we list some typical groupings:

1. Financial
2. Personnel
3. Research and Development
4. Production
5. Marketing.

   1. Financial Information defines the international and external cash flow of the organization together with its external borrowings and loans.
   2. Personnel Information describes the staff situation and related personnel.
   3. Research and Development Information shows future areas of company's concern.
   4. Production Information greatly depends on the type of business; thus for a Television Broadcasting Company, this describes the programmes being produced and transmitted and the resources used in these activities.
   5. Marketing Information indicates the sales situation and the efforts being made to promote a company's products.

The growth of data and information processing is directly related to the growth of an organization. The effective operation and control of an organization requires effective production and processing of information. Information systems produce data to satisfy the needs of management, as well as of parties external to the organization.

The information system designed to carry out this role in a modern organization consists of two major components:

1. The internal information system; and
2. The strategic information system.

Each of these components of the total system, serves one of the major tasks of management. Internal information reflects the internal activities of the organization such as its competitive actions, its environmental and sociological interests, its adaptation to political and financial trends. Strategic information must suggest what happened, what is happening and, perhaps, most important of all, what will happen. Both kinds of information are equally required in private industry, educational institutions, governmental agencies, the military, hospitals and various other organizations.

SIGNIFICANCE OF INFORMATION IN ONGC

Soon after Independence, the Government of India formulated a national policy which made development of the country's oil resources, the exclusive responsibility of the State.

As a first step towards the implementation of this policy, a Petroleum Division was created in October 1955 (exclusively for oil exploration in the country) within the Geological Survey of India. Soon the Division grew into the Directorate of Oil and Natural Gas, which was raised to the status of a Commission on August 14, 1956. The Commission was converted into a statutory body on October 15, 1959, with Headquarters at Tel Bhawan, Dehra Dun.

Beginning from a modest production-level of 0.04 million metric tonnes in 1961-1962, ONGC has succeeded in producing 26.26 million tonnes of crude oil and 241.800 tonnes of LPG in 1984-1985. The crude oil production for 1985-1986 is estimated to exceed 27 million tonnes. The Commission's gross profit for 1984-1985 stood at Rs. 1627.41 crores and after tax it was Rs. 882.41 crores, making ONGC the highest profit-earning public sector undertaking in India. Over 41,591 employees of ONGC belonging to various disciplines, are today actively engaged in the ceaseless search for oil[3].

In its role as India's major public enterprise for exploration and production of oil and natural gas, ONGC has within a span of 29 years, built up a sonnd base for achieving self-sufficiency in oil and natural gas and self-reliance in technology.

In ONGC, there seems to be no end to the process of information generation. A large volume of information, earlier generated has gone into the waste paper basket. The result is that "learning from facts" is incomplete even today. The planning is not sound. Management is not in a position to monitor and control. With the passage of time, the flow of information has increased manifold; and the gap between the flow of information and its utilization for management is ever widening. Therefore, in today's context, for organizations like ONGC, the the computer appears to be the only significant tool for for advances in management and for a productivity boost. Now a computer can do only what it has been instructed to do. Therefore, there has to be a careful selection of programmers, who are well versed in the affairs of the organization, for which the computer system has been designed. The system is not an end; it can only provide the means to achieve organizational objectives. Therefore, it has to be tailored to suit to organization's objectives and problems.

The internal component of the information systems supports the internal management and administration of the organization. It coordinates and integrates information generated by completely specific information systems (*i.e.*, those tailored to solve only certain specific problems) with the need for that information by systems related to other parts of the organization. The internal information system sorts out the information obtained and provides it in an easily understood form for use in strategic planning. In other words, the basic role of the system is to facilitate and enhance the flow of internal information within the organisation.

The internal information system in ONGC consists of a number of parts:

1. The completely specified systems
2. The common data base
3. The management reporting system
4. The information retrieval system; and
5. The data management system.

Figgure 10.1 depicts the internal information system in ONGC.

These individual parts of the internal information system supports the key managerial activity of operations control. They are basic building blocks on which the whole design and implementation of the internal information system is based. Most of the data vital to the routine administrative and operational activities of ONGC exists in completely specified information systems. Much of the information necessary for higher level decision-making results from the summarization and aggregation of this original mass of basic data.

Summary data and information from the completely specified systems appear at the individual interfaces and are transferred into the common data base. This data base acts as a centeal repository and exchange facility in ONGC. Data and

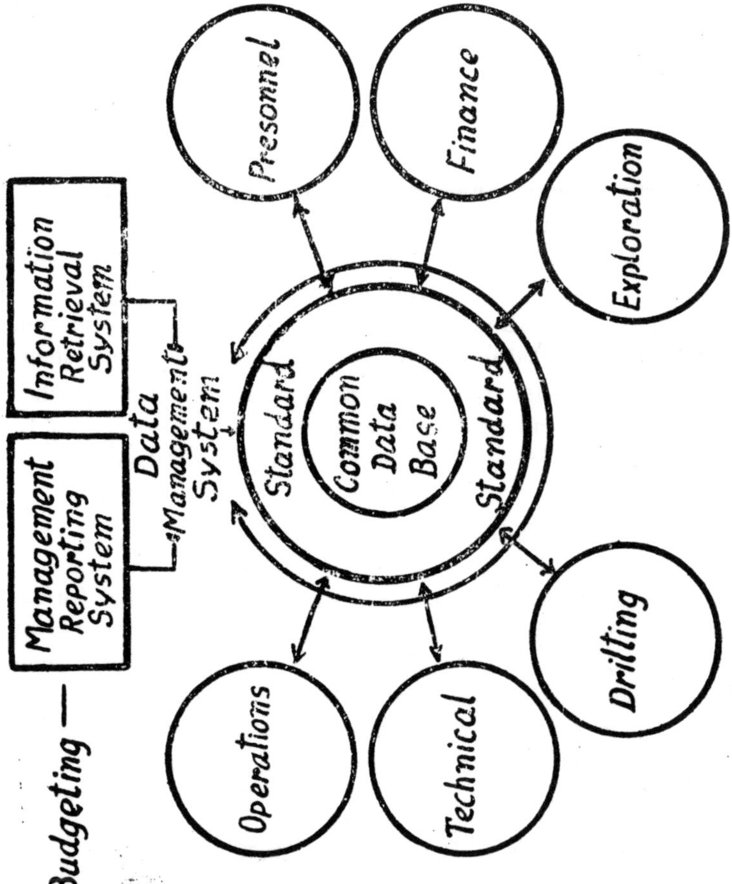

Fig. 10.1: Internal Information System in ONGC

information entering the common data base must be in a standard form that can be understood and used by all parts of the Commission.

Reports required for effective management control are compiled from data and information contained in the common data base. Reports such as financial statements which are needed at regular intervals are assembled by the management reporting system. This system deals only with reports that are to be presented in a previously designed format, on a regular and periodic basis. Other information needed in management control but not included in the structured, periodic reports can be provided to managers on demand by a specially designed information retrieval system in the Commission. The flow of data and information throughout the internal information system is controlled in ONGC by the data management system. The function of the data management system is to link together the various parts of the internal information system and to ensure the smooth operation of the whole organization.

FLOW OF INFORMATION

To facilitate and foster the flow of information through formal channels within organization is one of the major purposes of the internal information system. While fulfilling its formal function, the information system also often stimulates informal communication at the same time. However, its prime concern is with the formal passage of information between the parts of an organization the need to communicate with one another in the course of their day-to-day activities. The greater proportion of that communication is usually in the vertical direction, representing information flow from lower to higher levels in the organization, and *vice versa*. However, some part of the cömmunication is also in the horizontal direction, among individuals at the same level in the organizational hierarchy.

Information generally flows in organizations along two specific sets of paths: between individual officers having the same specialized function, such as personnel, accounting or production; and between responsibility centres set up to carry out specific tasks or projects[4]. The overall flow of information in a modern organization usually consists of a combination of the above types. The dominant flow in any organization is determined by the style of management adopted by the organization, and the authority structure and reporting procedures that have been set up to serve that management style.

In ONGC, there is a Board of Directors or "Commission Members", with the Chairman at the head. Each Member deals with a special wing of the Commission's business and has a separate Management Services Group (MSG) subordinate to him to look after his office at headquarters. The MSG to the Chairman is called the Corporate MSG. At Regional level, General Managers or Chief General Managers are top officials who have their own MSGs to support them in performing their assigned tasks. All these MSGs are interlinked.

Figure 10.2 shows the actual position.

The MSGs also look after the Management Information Systems (MIS) which convey accurate and timely information

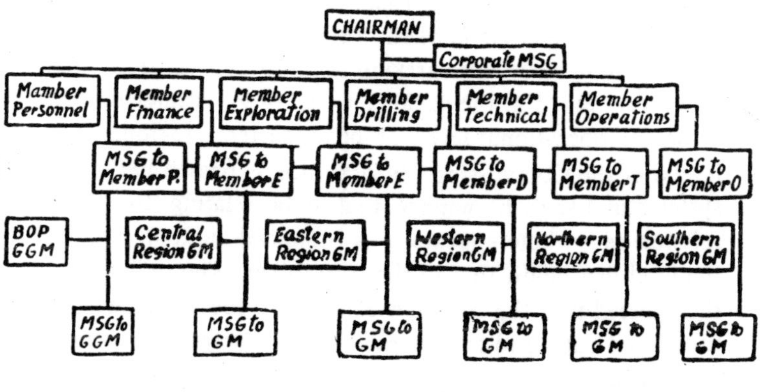

Fig. 10.2 : Chart shows Top Officials and their separate MSGs both at Headquarter and Regional Level

to the Chairman and to Members to enable them to make correct decisions about the future destiny of the Commission.

The media of information transmission in ONGC are mainly telephones, telexes, hotlines, computers and formal and informal reports. Data is received in the form of floppies, tapes and reports from internal sources and external agencies. At headquarters, it is compiled and processed partly by hand and partly by electronic devices. Information in the form of reports is then sent to the users. But a survey has indicated that more computers need to be installed both for business and scientific applications. Hence 1990, ONGC will have a perfectly computerized Management Information System (MIS).

Information is indispensable for decision-making in any organization in this age of rapid change and development—both social and technological. In ONGC, the emphasis is often placed on generating information flow along specialized functional lines. The usual information flow in ONGC, where specialist functions are predominant, resembles a conventional organization chart where most of the formal flow of information is in vertical direction. Information from the specialized functions is combined for the purposes of management control, primarily at the level of the Chairman. Hotizontal flow of information at all levels is usually fot liaison purposes only. In Figure 10.1 the circle marked "Finance" can be envisaged as a series of nested systems carrying out the specialized financial functions needed at the various levels (*e.g.*, strategic, tactical, technical, operational levels or headquarters, regional, project levels) of the Commission. Information is passed between these systems in a such a manner that data relating to the Commission as a whole appears at a financial system interface at the level just below that of the Chairman. The information is then passed into the common data base, combined with other functional data, and incorporated into management reports at the topmost level.

Figure 10.3 shows the information flow by specialized functions in ONGC.

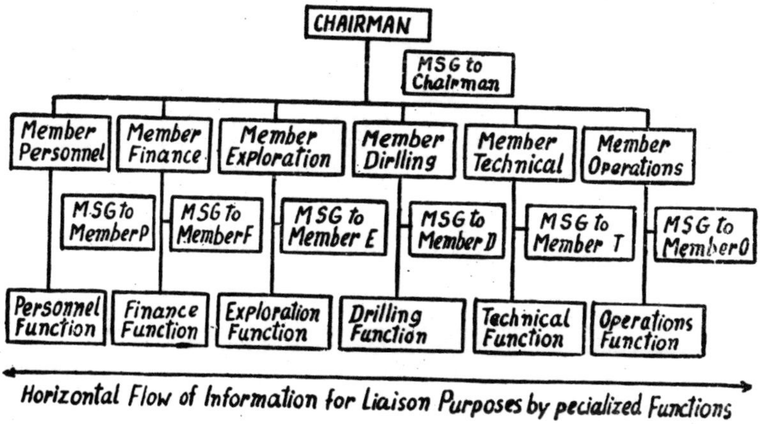

Fig. 10.3 : Chart showing Flow of Information at Headquarters of ONGC

Along with the above mentioned path of information flow, ONGC has also set up responsibility centres to deal with specific tasks as they arise. These responsibility centres are, in fact, miniature organizations themselves. They incorporate many specialized functional activities within their own management structure.

The emphasis is an organization consisting of a network of responsibility centres is normally placed on expenditing information flow between the centres. The information passed is inter-functional in nature rather than related to separate specialized functions. Communication between the specialized functions in the various responsibility centres is correspondingly less.

Information flow in ONGC structured by responsibility centres is shown in Fig. 10.4.

In this figure. five responsibility centres or regions are shown, each reporting to headquarters for projects falling in

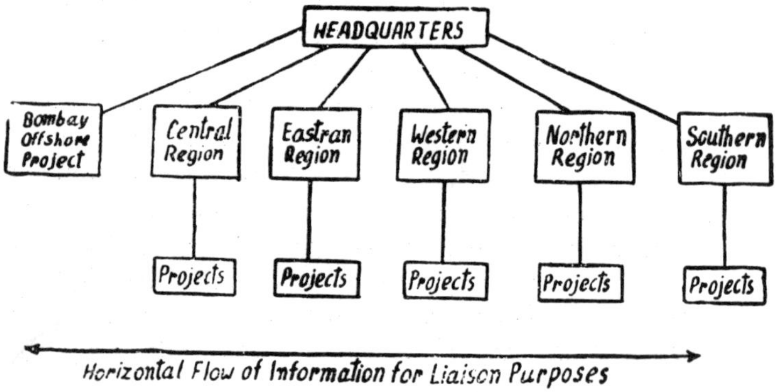

Fig. 10.4 : Information Flow by Responsibility Centres in ONGC.

their respective regions. Bombay Offshore Project (BOP) is also a responsibility centre. The information is passed from the inter faces to a common data base for the regions. Reports based on a combination of data from each function are used in the management control of the region. Formal communications within the Commission consist of exchanges between the common data bases in the various regions. Data exchanged between common data bases in regions must adhere to the standard set for the Commission's overall data base. Figure 10.4 depicts the information flow in ONGC by responsibility centres.

The data base is clearly a significant factor in formal communications between the various parts of the Commission. A substantial portion of the formal communications between the regions is made up of exchanges between the data bases at the various locations. Note that these communications occur not only between those in the direct line of authority, at various levels in the Commission, but also in different regions at the same level.

The Commission's overall data base is, therefore, clearly hierarchical in nature. This fact that any particular data is always stored in the same form regardless of its location in the Commission, considerably enhances communication between regions. In fact, the greater the degree of standardization achieved between the contents of the data base stored in the various locations; the greater is the potential for for communication between the various regions.

If the Chairman needs some information, his MSG will obtain it for him. Similarly, if any member needs information, he will inform his MSG and they will make the needed information available to him, after contacting the right person. Thus, if the Chairman wants to know how many drilling rigs are being used at a particular site and how many metres are being drilled in a specific time period, the corporate MSG will ask the MSG of the Member (Drilling) for this information. The MSG to Member (D) will contact the MSG of the official concerned with the particular project and make accurate and timely information available to the Corporate MSG.

Conclusion

Information is an essential commodity in all modern activities. Individuals, organizations and communities use information in every sphere of their day-to-day affairs. Most organizations have some sort of information system to handle and process the information needed in their work.

Information flow in an organization may be through either formal channels. The "internal information system" is concerned with the formal part of the flow. The formal information flow may be in the "vertical" direction between hierachic levels in the organization or in the "horizontal" direction between individuals and offices at roughly the same level. Information often flows between individual officers with the same specialized function. It may also flow between responsibility centres through the formal authority structure. In practical cases, the flow information usually consists of a mix of both of these, dictated by the style of management adopted in the organizations.

NOTES AND REFERENCES

1. Lucas, H. C., Jr. : Information Systems Concepts for Management. New York, McGraw-Hill Book Company, 1978, p. 15.
2. Davis, Gordon B. : Management Information systems : Conceptual Foundation, Structure and Development. New York, McGraw-Hill Book Company 1974, p. 32.
3. ONGC Diary, 1986.
4. Redford, K. J. : Information Systems for Strategic Decisions. Virginia, Reston Publishing Company, Inc., 1978, pp. 99-103.

11

Governmental Records 'Explosion' —Measures to Contain It

K.D. MADAN

Much of the history of human civilization relating even to times long before the use of script was known to man or paper was invented, is contained in some sort of records. Clay tablets of ancient Babylon, Egyptian murals, dried skin and inscriptions on papyrus scrolls, all bear evidence to man's propensity to, and reliance on, record keeping.

In modern day world, in the governmental establishments as well as industrial and commercial organisations, big or small, need is constantly felt to determine and record a vast number of facts both in day to day discharge of their functions and for use in future. Much of this recorded information is of course intended to be retrieved in course of time for effective decision making. The efficiency and effectiveness of any organisation depends to a large extent on the right information becoming available to it readily at the right time.

In governmental affairs, several factors such as accountability to people through their representatives in parliament, requirements of audit, varying legal requirements in different situatians, and considerations of equity and fairness which in turn desiderate consistency and uniformity in decisions in similar cases necessitate proper maintenance of recorcs. This presupposes the existence of a competent system of records management in the government.

Unfortunately, however, records management has been a relatively neglected field and has usually received a low priority in the list of tasks to be accomplished by the administrators, work-a-day as most of them are. On the other hand, mounting piles of records in the secretariat year after year have brought about a situation which could perhaps be described as 'records explosion' and which demands instant as well as constant attention.

The problem is not confined to India alone. In some of the western countries. the realisation of this problem dawned years ago. In the U.K., in 1952, the British Government set up a Committee under the chairmanship of Sir James Grigg to review the arrangements for preservation of records of the government departments. In its report which the Committee submitted in 1954, it observed that the public records already transferred to the Public Record Office (counterpart of the National Archives here) which, according to the Committee, covered a period of nearly a thousand years, occupied over 200,000 ft. (or about 40 miles). of shelf space. This Committee also estimated that the records in possession of the various government departments which would ultimately be transferred to the Public Record Office for permanent preservation would require 600,000 ft. of shelf space (or about 120 miles). In other words, the amount of preservable material with the various departments would be about three times the quantum of preserved material already in the custody of the Public Record Office. The Committee recalled that a previous inquiry into the arrangements for preservation of public records had been undertaken by the Royal Commission on Public Records appointed as far back as in 1910. It also observed that the wide extension of the field of government business in the twentieth century and the invention of such devices as the typewriter and the duplicating machines had increased enormously the pace of creation of departmental records.

Five years earlier, in 1947, the U.S. government had set up a commission on organisation of the Executive Branch of the Government. This Commission in turn set up several task forces including one on records management. The task force on records management estimated that in 1940, approximately 18.5 million cubic feet of federal records occupied more than 18 million sq. ft. of shelf space costing "not less than $ 27 million annually". The space occupied by federal records was found by the task force to be equivalent to six times the size of the Pentagon.

The Government of Canada set up a Royal Commission on Government Organisation in 1960. This Commission, in volume I of its report on management of the public service, estimated that about $ 500 million was spent on paper work which was about 1/12 of the total budget of 1961. According to the Commission, at least 2.5 million cubic feet of records were stored in government premises and each year 250,000 cubic feet were being added. This latter volume of records, the Commission graphically equated to the carrying capacity of 83 railway box cars. The Commission further lamented that 10 miles of shelf space was being added only to hold new books and publications being acquired by the various government departments. Describing the nature of the problem, the Commission observed thus: "Mounting tide of paper can inundate the public service unless management pays strict attention to regulating its flow and directing it into useful channels. Records have a life cycle. They are conceived, brought into the world, live a more or less purposeful life in active files, tend to reproduce themselves and in old age are decently cared for in dormant storage. When they have no purpose to serve, they are cremated. Haphazard control of any stage in the life cycle can be disasterous in so massive an operation."

In India too, to realisation seems to have come more or less the same time with the publication of the report of the Committee on Archival Legislation (better known as Tara Chand Committee) (1960). This Committee observed that the holdings of records of the various central ministries alone covered more than 21,000 linear feet of space (about 40 miles). The Committee estimated that the subordinate offices had in their custody in addition 'even on a modest view' records needing about 176 linear miles of shelf space. According to this Committee, the annual overall rate of accrual of records in the various offices was about 41,000 linear ft. (or about 8 miles) which meant that the Government would need each year a new repository almost half the size of the National Archives building. Furthermore, since the central departments were fast multiplying, the growth of central records was taking place almost in a geometrical progression. The Committee expressed its dismay by saying, "that any hope of the centre being able to provide for the upkeep of all its records is likely to prove illusory."

A few years later, the Estimates Committee (1968-69) of the Lok Sabha expressed serious concern about the problem of mounting of records and in particular the immediate need of appraisal of old and semi-current records and suggested a measures to overcome the problem. In the words of the Estimates Committee:

> "Considering the voluminous records requiring appraisal which are estimated to be in the neighbourhood of 240 linear miles, it is necessary that a phased programme for the completion of this work over a period of time should be prepared as early as possible and necessary staff deployed for the purpose. The Committee need hardly point out that appraisal of records in time is essential for proper record management; it serves a two-fold purpose—it helps in the weeding of unwanted papers resulting in saving of space on the one hand, and in the proper preservation of permanent valuable records, on the other. The Committee urge that no further time should be lost in drawing up a phased pro-

gramme for appraisal as suggested above and implementing the same in right earnest".

It would be seen that in a short span of eight years from the time the Tara Chand Committee went into the problem to the time that the Estimates Committee of the Lok Sabha addressed itself to the matter, the volume of records—non-current and semi-current—had gone up six times *i.e.*, from 40 linear miles to 240 linear miles of shelf space. In other words, an annual accrual roughly at the rate of 25 linear miles of shelf space was taking place. Considering that the National Archives of India has only about 80,000 linear ft. or about 15 miles of shelf space, the Government of India would require repository about 18 times the size of the National Archives of India for its non-current and semi-current records and in addition a new repository about one and a half times the size of the National Archives every year to hold its records. The problem in the Union Territories and States closely resembles the one at the Centre and in some cases is even worse than that.

At this point, it appears necessary to interrupt the narrative concerning the dimensions of the problem, in order that we may have a clear idea as to what the terms 'semi-current' and 'non-current' connote so far as records are concerned. When any record is created, it is for a specified purpose in day-to-day administration. Until that purpose is finally achieved or is abandoned, the record can be said to be in the stage of currency. Once that stage is reached the next stage is that of the file being 'recorded' either with or without any indication of:

(a) how long it would be maintained?

(b) a re-examination at the end of the prescribed period and

(c) weeding out of valueless material.

While still retained by the creating agency, this may be termed as in the stage of 'semi-currency'. The files at this stage may be either quite active during this period or they may be comparatively non-active, depending upon the contents of the files, the thinking of the government and of the agency concerned. The crucial point, however, is that they are no longer required for the purpose for which they were originally created, but only for ancillary services to other transactions. That such semi-current records should be segregated from the current records is obvious. Finally, comes the stage when the semi-current files become non-active for administrative purposes. By that time, material of ephemeral interest has been weeded out. They are no longer required for reference by the creating agencies, at least not frequently enough to warrant their being further retained by the creating agencies. The stage of records is referred to as 'non-current'. When records have attained this stage, they are ripe enough to be tranferred to the appointed places in record rooms to be kept as non-current records for indefinite retention. In course of time, they would be subjected to periodical appraisal and those of enduring value would, at the appropriate time, be sent to the National Archives.

In his sixth report (relating to the year (1978-79) on the implementation of the Archival Policy Resolution, the Director of Archives has reported that in 1978-79, in 634 out of the total of 740 central Ministries/Departments and other offices which furnished the data, about 16 to 17 lakhs of non-current records were awaiting final appraisal. Earlier some 14½ lakhs of files had been accessioned to the National Archives without final appraisal. The figure non-current files which were awaiting final appraisal in March 1979 thus exceeded 31 lakhs. (In March 1976, the corresponding figure was 25 lakhs.) This is a huge figure by any reckoning, but the position of semi-current records is even worse. The 634 agencies referred to earlier had in their possession more than 2.8 crore files, 4 lakh registers, 37 lakh bills, 40,000 bound volumes, 536 bundles, 3 lakh charts, 65 lakh cards in addition to thousands of running ledger accounts, books and other types of records, in all totalling more than 4 crores of documents tied up in bundles or just lying loose. On a rough estimate, 80 per cent of these semi-current records, after a proper review by the records creating agencies themselves, could be disposed of making room for accommodating fresh accruals of recorded files.

Needless to say, these piles of semi-current and non-current records occupying valuable space both in the National Archives of India and central ministries/offices are costing millions of rupees per year to the exchequer. According to a costing attempted by the National Archives a couple of years ago, the rent of space to provide shelving for one file in metropolitan cities like Delhi, Bombay and Calcutta was about Rs. 1 per year to the exchequer. With the recent hike in rental values in these cities this cost could safely be put at Rs. 1.50 per file today. The problem having not only attained, but well passed menacing proportions, the need therefore for launching a crash programme for management of records on scientific lines not only in the N.A.I. and the central ministries/departments but also in the States and Union Territories is obvious and crying.

It must be stated here straightway that there is no dearth of instructions in this regard. Firstly, there is the Manual of Office Procedure which lays down detailed instructions in regard to systematic filing of papers, indexing and recording of files and the custody, review and weeding out of non-current records. These instructions *inter alia* cover classification of records according to their importance from historical and administrative viewpoints, formulation of records retention schedules, and control mechanisms to keep a watch on records proliferation. Various OMs have been issued in amplification of these instructions from time to time.

Alongside of the instructions laid down in the Manual of Office Procedure, there is the Archival Policy Resolution issued by the Government of India in 1972. This lays stress on the need for departmental record rooms, suitable training for the officers in charge of such departmental record rooms, and the timely transfer of records selected for permanent preservation to the National Archives 25 years after their being closed or recorded. It also prescribes instructions for compilation and periodical revision of retention schedules, and of the organisational history of each department. The responsibilities of the Director of Archives, and particularly his coordinating and guiding role with respect to public records, etc. are also set out in the Resolution.

The gravamen of the instructions contained in the Manual of Office Procedure and the Policy Resolution is that whatever record is unnecessary may be destroyed; whatever has some value for the future should be classified carefully and preserved but even this latter category should be subjected to periodical reviews so that at the time of each review, the value of the record for further preservation can be appraised and only when it is found that a certain record is of permanent value whether from a historical angle or from the administrative point of view, should it be consigned to the National Archives of India.

Notwithstanding this, however, it would be seen from the earlier part of this article that the aforesaid instructions are being honoured more in their breach than in actual observance. It is indeed not as if by the mere fact of appraisals and reviews by the various ministries and departments now and again the, problem can reach a solution. Quite obviously, since the problem must be contained within manageable dimensions and since only such records must be preserved as have intrinsic value from historic as well as administrative angles, a prepondering proportion of the piles of non-current records which do not answer to this description must be promptly identified and then forthwith destroyed. Unless this is done, the chaff would not be separated from the grain which too must continue to perish until then. It has to be appreciated that the whole purpose behind the archival preservation of records is that what is worthwhile should not only be retained but be easily retrievable so as to be available to the historian, researcher and the administrator. This is possible only if it can be segregated at the earliest possible stage from all that is worthless and of no consequence in the rest of the heap. If this cannot be accomplished at the earliest stage, the whole lot will get more and more intermingled not only involving much greater difficulty in segregating it later, but also involving the possibility that what might have been of permanent value would get submerged in the mass of worthless stuff and become impossible of being picked out later. In fact one could go a step further, namely, that if the problem is to be contained for the future, the urgent need for leafing through and weeding out of even current record from the time one gets created so as to put a halt to this ever-growing mound needs hardly any emphasis.

In his latest report (relating to 1978-79) on the implementation of the Archival Policy Resolution, the Director of Archives while complaining of the present tendency of the ministries to push their non-current redords to the National Archieves of India without prior appreisal, has also mentioned that the drawing up of the retention schedules of the various ministries/departments themselves is also in arrears. The Director of Archives has however rightly stressed that the drawing up of the schedules themselves is not enough; what is important is its actual implementation.

The Director of Archives has also, in the aforesaid report, lamented the lack of an archival law for which, in his rekoning. an Archival Policy Resolution is no substitute. This is arguable. If the provisions of the Archival Policy Resolution have not so far been implemented, the lack of implementation cannot be attributed to want of statutory authority but to a total lack of appreciation on the part of ministries/departments of the magnitude of the problem and of the importance of proper records management. The Policy Resolution has, in fact, the merit of flexibility so that any changes, the need for which might become apparent from time to time, can be introduced with relative ease. Legislation no doubt imposes a legal obligation. But at the same time it introduces a rigidity in procedure which militates against expediency and innovation—attributes needed most in a crisis situation like the present one. In any case, the mere enactment of legislation by itself is unlikely to make the ministries and departments alive to the situation if the Policy Resolution has not.

What seems the first and foremost step in this direction is to arouse consciousness among the ministries and departments and the staff working in them particularly those concerned with the management of records about the ever growing volume of records, or the records 'explosion' as described earlier, the urgent need to separate the chaff from the grain and to consign outright the former to the incinerator, or in other words, to undertake their outright destruction. Perhaps campaigns and drives to do away with unwanted records in the same way as, and perhaps more vigorously than, the campaigns we have launched to clear the arrears at frequent intervals interspersed with seminars, workshops and discussions within ministries, departments, offices and in fact even individual divisions and sections of offices, to arouse the consciousness of all concerned, may be the starting point to clean up the Augean stables. This arousal of consciousness and awakening in the records creating agencies, particularly among the higher echelons, could serve as the initial impetus or impulse and turn out to be highly rewarding even if in the early stages spectacular results may not be discernible.

This may be followed if not accompanied, by the setting up of control mechanism in the shape of special cells to be installed in each ministry/department to oversee the progress of the work of appraisal and weeding of records under the direct supervision of the Secretary of the Ministry or the head of the department, with the latter bestowing his personal attention to this. The progress report should indicate the total quantum of records appraised, those intended to be weeded out, and actually weeded out, those to be retained as also the remaining holdings of records yet to be reviewed. This in fact is a business which for quite some time to come would need no less attention than the actual day-to-day business being transacted if we are not to be overtaken by the deluge referred to in the opening paragraphs of this paper.

No less important is the existence of a well-organised departmental record room in each ministry and department where records can remain in a state of good preservation. Due to paucity of space in most offices, huge piles of records are kept in highly unsatisfactory surroundings devoid of infrastructure facilities like proper shelves and other essential equipment like fire extinguishers, exhaust fans and spraying machines, etc., to ensure proper dusting, spraying and repair of records. Out of the 46 central government organisations which furnished information to the Director of Archives on the question whether proper record room facilities were available, as many as 25 stated that record rooms were not properly equipped. These included even important ministries like Defence and Labour, Departments of Civil Supplies and Co-operation, Company Affairs. Expenditure, Power, Office of the Director General of Health Services, Union Public Service Commission, and so on, all in Delhi and several offices situated outside Delhi. Several other organisations which sent information simply reported that they did not have any provision for housing of their records, The provision of a scientifically organised departmental record room for every ministry and office is indeed a must for ensuring the proper unkeep of records during the long spells of time for which these have to be kept by the creating agencies.

Equally important is the need for training those in charge of management of records and particularly the officers in charge of the departmental record rooms. The latter are usually, or should be. whole time staff for the purpose of records management. The National Archives of India has been organising short-term in service training courses in archival management since 1973-74, intended *inter alia* for officers manning the various departmental record rooms in the central ministries and offices. For the past two years or so they have also been running, correspondence courses for this purpose. These are certificate courses. In addition to these regular courses, special facilities for observation-cum-training in records management, repair of records and micro-filming are also provided by the National Archives of India. What is urgent is that each ministry and department should get a nucleus of staff speedily trained in this highly important discipline.

Side by side it ought to be possible for the Internal Work Study Units in the various ministries and in fact the Staff Inspection Unit, to look into the question of staff requirements for departmental record rooms of various size depending upon the quantum of record holdings so as to be able to prescribe a uniform pattern of staffing of this highly important wing in each office.

There is also an urgent need for preparation of comprehensive archival manual which would contain not only the principles and practices of modern records management and the requirements of the Archival Policy Resolution, but also the provisions of the Manual of Office Procedure concerning, filing, indexing, classification, appraisal review, maintenance preservation and weeding out of records. The manual could with advantage contain provisions regarding the qualitative aspect of records management and also educational and other qualifications and professional expertise required for each functionary working in the departmental record rooms. This comprehensive and self-contained manual should be distributed to all officers in charge of departmental record room as well as to all O & M officers of each ministry and department.

To sum up, the rate at which records in government are multiplying should be a matter for serious concern to all. Despite the fact that the committees appointed by the Government as also the Estimates Committee of Parliament, had spelt out the magnitude of the problem with clarity, little impact seems to have been made on the quarters concerned. What is called for is immediate active involvement of the top echelons in various ministries and departments and the launching of special campaigns and drives for not only weeding out the unwanted records but also to put into place the wanted records in an organised and easily retrievable fashion so that they can be of use at the required time to the decision maker, the research worker or the historian. Measures to arouse to consciousness at senior levels to the rapidly growing problem, setting up of suitable control mechanisms to oversee the progress of appraisal of non-current and semi-current records, providing proper departmental record rooms in each ministry/department with the required infrastructural facilities like proper shelves and equipment, imparting proper training to personnel in charge of management of records and laying down of norms for staffing the departmental record rooms can brook no furtherdelay. Last but not the least, the preparation of a comprehensive archival manual needs to be taken up on an urgent basis.

BIBLIOGRAPHY

Records Management in the United State Government—A Report with recommendations—Prepared for the Commission on Organisation of the Executive Branch of the Government—United States Government, January 1949.

Committee on Departmental Records—Report—Her Majesty's Stationery Office, July 1954;

Management of the Public Service, The Royal Commission on Government Organisation, Canada, 1962.

Manual of Office Procedure (Eighth Edition), Government of India, Department of Personnel and Administrative Reforms, October 1978.

Report of the Committee on Archival Legislation, National Archives of India, 1960.

Estimates Committee (1968-69-Fourth Lok Sabha), Sixty-Ninth Report—Ministry of Education—National Archives of India—Lok Sabha Secretariat.

Report of the Records Management Committee—National Archives of India, June 1976.

Sixth Report of the Director of Archives on the Implementation of the Archival Policy Resolution—1978-79, National Archives of India, 1979.

12

Public Relations for Financial Management

History and Development

According to J. Derriman, writing in 1969, public relations practice is the deliberate, planned and sustained effort to establish and maintain mutual understanding between an organisation and its public.[1] Writing a decade later with George Pulay, he saw public relations as building a bridge of understanding, acceptance and goodwill between the company and its audience.[2] All public relations seeks to create a better understanding between companies and their public through the presentation of the correct company message, at the right time, in the right place, and presented in the right manner. The communications tools of public relations apply equally to financial public relations, but here the similarity ends. It was once said that the general public relations practitioner.

> ...would feel he had the armoury capable of doing the job without knowing what the job is. He doesn't understand the nicety of the market place.

Financial public relations is a specialist activity, not only because of the complexity of its subject matter but also because of the nature of its audience. The audience can be as large as the adult population' of the United Kingdom, or as geographically widespread as the international investing community, and it can be as small and narrow as 150 specialist investment analysts, fund managers and financial journalists. For financial institutions, public relations is the 'below-line' marketing of money products, such as life assurance, unit trusts, building society investments, to the media who filter and disseminate information on saving and investment schemes to the public. For the corporate sector, financial public relations is a vital segment in a company's communications. It is the presentation of information and viewpoints on a company's financial, industrial and commercial activities to the financial and investing community, to financial journalists and to the public.

Today, public relations and financial public relations people are a confident group who feel no need to apologise for their existence. Financial public relations is now part of the formal range of City services and is used by most large firms in the corporate sector. In 1983 there were, according to the Public Relations Year Book, 114 public relations firms of which 35 offered specialist services in financial public relations. It was estimated that nearly 2,000 people were employed in agency/consultancy public relations work. The firms are highly competitive or, as the economist would argue, in a state of perfect competition. The average number of employees to a firm is just over thirteen. There is only one firm with over 100 employees and 115 firms employ under twenty persons.

The foundation of formal public relations as expressed by a trade asssociation and other formal appendages belongs to the post-war period. It was not until 1948 that the Institute of Public Relations was established as the trade association for in-house corporate public relations officers and their counterparts in agencies. It was only in 1969 that consultants and agency practitioners became represented by the Public Relations

Consultants Association which in 1983 counted 96 UK members. The first independent specialist financial public relations agency, Angel Court Consultants, formed by R. Sitwell, R. Sachs and P. Syrett, was not established until 1960. The City Communication Centre, established in 1976, marks the formal recognition by the City that its image (or the needs of its institutions) had to be projected and that their views must be put forward in an organised way. Only in the 1960s was the PRO seedy image of 'suede shoes dipped in gin' gradually replaced by professionalism. For during this time the communicator became more prominent, supplying the increased information demanded by the Companies Act and the Stock Exchange and by increasing corporate and takeover activity. In the 1970s public relations emerged with a strategic advisory capability and with this chauge in role, came the acceptance of public relations as a profession in spite of the fact that there is no specific graduate or post-graduate course in any university or polytechnic in the United Kingdom.

Whilst the formal institutions of public relations have a comparatively short life, the practice of public relations has a longer history. In-house public relations in the corporate sector developed in the inter-war years. It was largely a response to necessity. For example, in 1930 Henry Mond and the public relations staff of ICI succeeded in obtaining a renewal of the Dyestuff Act.[3] The ICI education sponsorship programme of 1927 was largely a response to its recruitment problems. Pilkington appointed Pritchard & Partners as public relations consultants as early as 1928 at a time of severe competition from foreign manufacturers of flat drawn glass and on the eve of the launch of a new special glass called Vita glass.[4] The adoption of publicity managers and public relation officers by the corporate sector was largely influenced by the demonstration of their value in government departments and public institutions during the First World War. By 1938, in-house public relations was sufficiently significant for the PEP Report on the Press to devote some space to it. The report observed:

A good example of the power of public relations is the very great change in attitude of the Press to the railways.

It noted the growth in industrial and commercial news in the newspapers as a response to increased public demand. This was facilitated by the supply of news items or feature articles supplied by a company's publicity department, by an advertising or press agency or, more rarely, produced on the initiative of the advertisement manager of the newspaper. It observed that the better treatment of some companies in the press was a result of the trained publicity managers now employed by many of the leading industrial firms and advertisers and concluded:

> The increasing practice of appointing public relations officers and publicity managers has contributed to industry's influence on the Press.
>
> Finally, upon the merits of public relations, it observed:
>
> It is shown elsewhere in this Report how hastily and inexpertly news, and particularly specialised news, can be handled in a newspaper office. The employment of an expert, therefore, to guard against such errors by supplying news written up in a suitable form for the Press, and to rectify them, is not merely a legitimate act of self-defence on the part of a firm or industry but is often a positive help to the Press.[5]

The Second World War made public relations respectable. Information officers came out at the end of the war as communicators and, in many cases, joined large public companies.[6] Another factor in the post-war growth in public relations was the example set by the in-house public relations departments of American multinational companies operating in the United Kingdom. Nevertheless, general public relations, as practised in the 1950s, was not much different from that practised before the war. It was still relatively crude and limited, as noted by Rene Elvin of Crawfords, in an article in the Financial Times of 25 January, 954;

> In Britain PR is all too often regarded merely as the means of obtaining free editorial publicity by way of handouts to the Press.

It was primarily concerned with circulating news to the press. On financial public relations, Elvin was a little harsh in his judgement when he wrote:

> Another function of public relations, still inadequately used in this country, is the cultivation of good-will among shareholders. Too many British companies still treat these as almost negligible quantities as long as satisfactory dividends ars paid.

The superior state of American 'investor relations' owed much to their open company structure under which companies can buy back their shares from existing shareholders. It is this which gave an extra dimension to their 'investor relations' activities. By contrast the 'closed' company structure of UK corporations locks this stimulus. Nevertheless listed public companies not only spent hundreds of pounds annually in informing their shareholders about the state of the company and its prospects in the form of chairman's speech and statement advertisements, but their agencies supplied the financial press with news items, financial results, board changes, new orders, etc.

Indeed, financial public relations, in the form of distributing financial news to the press in the hope of editorial mention, precedes general public relations. For example, Walter Skinner's financial news agency, established in 1866, distributed financial news itmes to the press from its earliest days. The nineteenth-century press devoted considerable editorial space to the financial reports of companies, covering not only the essential points of the directors' report but also the chairman's comments. It was the late nineteenth-century company promoter who first used public relations with the press. Some, like, H. Osborne O' Hagan, furnished the editorial staff of the financial press with financial news items.[7] At another level, to combat an avaricious financial press, company promoters paid out large sums of money to have their side of things presented. E.T. Hooley, a notorious company promoter, explained in his memoirs:

> At the time when I was promoting dozens of companies and when everything depended upon favourable criticism by financial writers, I spent a small fortune in paying hush money to people who had it in their power to do me harm.[8]

Moreover, at his bankruptcy hearing in 1898, Hooley claimed:

> I have promoted companies that I have not made a single penny out of, because the newspapers took all the profit. I have paid one alone £40,000. A single article in another paper cost me £10,000. As soon as it is known that a company is coming out I am besieged by them and their representatives.[9]

In these circumstances, financial public relations was operating at two levels. On the one hand it involved the distribution of company financil news to the press. On the other hand, payment was frequently required for favourable publicity, whilst a refusal to pay resulted in unfavourable editorial, whether justified or not. Finally, as we have already seen in a previous chapier, the firm of Walter Judd, even before the First World War, was producing favourable articles on particular companies and industries and engineering their publication as editorial in even that most august of newspapers, The Times. The achievement of public-relations-inspired articles remains today amongst the most coveted results of public relations. Therefore the story of financial public relations began in the nineteenth century and was largely confined to the new corporate sector, to new issues and the press.

The adoption of financial public relations by financial institutions of the City of London began only with the Stock Exchange in 1958, a quarter of a century later than in the New York Stock Exchange. As early as 1933 the New York Exchange initiated a plan to sell itself to the public through radio, press publicity, direct mail, lectures and film displays.[10] As early as 1942, suggested reforms of the Stock Exchange included a proposal to appoint a PRO to present the Stock Exchange to outside interests, particularly the press.[11] Even the devastating results of a Daily Express poll asking. Do you consider that the Stock Exchange performs a useful service in the life of the community?', to which only 29 per cent of the sample answered in the affirmative, failed to move the Stock Exchange in the appointment of a PRO. Share booms and occasional disasters gave the Stock Exchange some bad publicity in the late 1950s. Takeovers, the mushrooming of finance companies, property scandals and a new issue boom stimulated questions of shareholder protection. Moreover, many small investors had come within the orbit of the Stock Exchange under the impetus of economic expansion and the Wider Share Ownership movement. The expansion in new investors and the 'casino' image of the Stock Exchange led left-wing politicians and economists to demand that the Exchange reform itslf, or be reformed. The Stock Exchange reacted in a number of ways. In 1955, the Exchange produced the first publication of annual interest and dividend payments on all securities.[12] J.W. Thompson were appointed as public relations advisors. The results include the first of a series of films on the Exchange, 'My Word is my Bond' (1958), the appointment of Simon Preston as public relations officer and the opening of the public gallery. The Stock Exhange had finally bowed to outside pressure. It was forced to project an image, to educate the public about its role in society, tighten up its quotation rules for the protection of investors and provide statistical information on the amount of business handled.

It was also in 1958 that formal financial public relations

was adopted by a merchant bank. During the Aluminium takeover battle, in face, of complete intransigence and secrecy from the board of British Aluminium, Tube Investments and their advisers, S.G. Warburg, enlisted the help of financial journalists in an attempt to open the debate and put their case to a wider audience. This direct communication attempt to enlist the aid of the financial press brought not only welcome publicity for the offeree's case but established the value of public relations in a contested takeover bid. It is perhaps pertinent to point out that Warburgs was not established in London until after the Second World War and was for years viewed by City diehards as a new comer—a negative attribute in the City—while Tube Investments, a leading British metals firm, was a Midlands firm with its head office in Birmingham. Since that time financial public relations has been an essential element in takeovers. The Aluminium battle also acted as an impetus to the adoption of a new attitude among the merchant banks. Before the takeover battle, according to P. Ferris:

> With one or two exceptions the merchant banks share a distaste for publicity. Their reputation is what counts they say—and that, they argue, involves the exercise of absolute discretion. To have their name in the paper is agreeable only if it appears in a small discreet paragraph dealing with a new issue or a consortium.[13]

However, after the debacle of the Aluminium bid, in which Hambros' chairman, R. Olaf Hambro, attracted adverse publicity as joint leader of the city consortium opposing the Reynolds/Tube Investment bid, Hambros appointed the public relations firm of Patrick Dolan to handle the bank's publicity. Since that time, merchant banks have used financial public relations to promote themselves as well as their activities in corporate finance and in new issue work.

Editorial comment, which has the flavour of 'third party endorsement,' was just as much appreciated by the late nineteenth-century company promoter as his twentieth-cenuryt successors, the issuing houses and stockbrokers. The importance of favourable editorial comment and advertising to attract the attention of prospective investors has not diminished during this century. However, increasingly since the last war, the success or failure of a new issue has become largely determined by institutional investors. Financial public relations could be said to be not only the process of making the increasingly complex prospectus understandable but also the marketing of the company as an investment opportunity to prospective investors (see Fig. 12.1).

Beginning in 1981, the government's privatisation programme has added a new dimension to financial public relations in the new issue field. Not only is the size of such issues larger than usual, but projected future issues, according to the press, are very large indeed—for example, the £4bn sale of British Telecom, £3bn for British Gas, £500m for BP, as well as the possible flotation of the electricity and mining sectors. The very size of such issues present the issuing house and the communicators with particular problems of timing the issue and preparing the market. Then there is the problem associated with the very nature of nationalised industries. For over 30 years they have had no contact with the City, the government is their banker, they had no need to raise capital on the market or please shareholders with a rising line of dividends or capital gains from rising share values. Their operations have been constrained by social, rather than market considerations. A major task, therefore, is to establish and build communication links with the City. Moreover, it is part of the government's policy to widen the existing share-owning base, to inform and attract potential private investors. In a relatively short space of time, potential investors and their advisers have to be apprised of the history, status and future prospects of what are amongst the largest industries in the country. Such an educative campaign, beginning from scratch to build knowledge and change perceived attitudes, is an intense PR exercise. Moreover, the attitude of other, larger groups—the company's

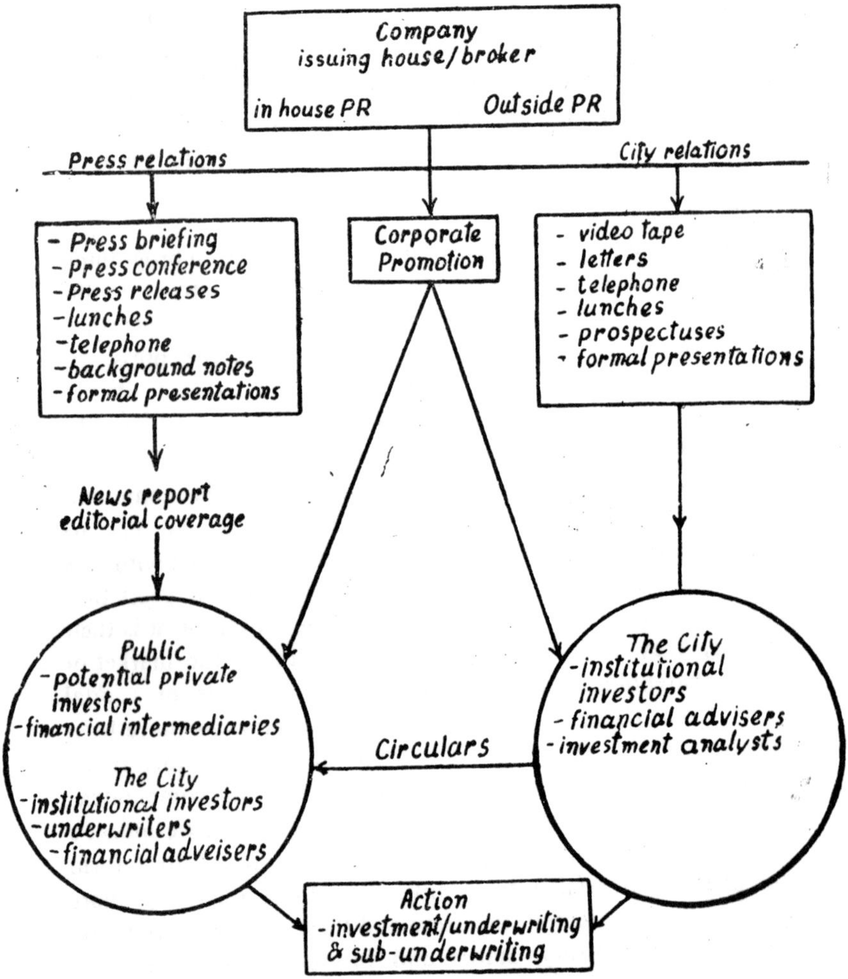

Fig. 12.1: Financial public relations in an offer for sale or public issue

employees, and the public—are areas for attitudal conversion as part of the government's call for a share-owning democracy.

The 1960s was the decade in which press relations, dealing with promotion of the company to soareholders via the press, saw a parallel growth of financial advertising. Financial journalists from the popular press moved into positions in agencies, and companies. Later they were followed by journalists from the quality press. The growth of public relations is exemplified by a growth in the number of agencies offering public relations services. Of the firms in existence today, 11 were established in the 1950s, 36 in the 1960s and 80 in the 1970s.[14] It was also seen in the growth of public relations departments in public companies. In the early 1960s Unilever, one of the largest companies in the United Kingdom, finally established an Information Unit at its headquarters in London and Rotterdam. Its function was defined as to protect, maintain and develop the good name of Unilever inside and outside the business by all legitimate means.'[15] However, financial public relations was already well established as Mr George Cale, chairman of Unilever, explained in his speech to shareholders in 1962:

> Much of the smooth functioning of the business depends on good communications and the passing-on of information... In this time of change, communications matter more than ever. If we do not keep you, the shareholders, and others of the general public well informed, then we have only ourselves to blame if your ideas of what we are and what we do get out of date.

He went on to make one of the most positive points of public relations:

> Good communications do not always make change palatable, but they do make it intelligible and they kill the wider rumours.[16]

In 1966, according to The Times' survey, there were 40

specialist public relations agencies in the United Kingdom sending company news direct to the press besides ten City financial advertising agencies, During the 1970s, financial public relations underwent two transformations. It moved from outside the board room (waiting for a press release and distributing it) to within the board room with an advisory strategic capacity. It moved from a defensive and reactive role to a creative, development role. Instead of being merely the executive arm of the decision-making process it became part of it. Financial public relations moved from being the poor relation to specialist professional status advising on the most efficient means of communication with an audience.

The expansion in financial communication since the 1960s in terms of:

1. the amount and quality of information companies provide to shareholders, investment analysis, fund managers and the public;
2. the depth and breadth of financial coverage in the press;
3. the increasing quality of stockbrokers' circulars and analysts' forecasts;
4. the rise of specialist financial public relation agencies and consultancies:
5. the adoption of in-house financial public relations spokesmen;
6. the rising status of financial communication as a function of senior management;
7. the establishment of corporate information departments, public affairs department or a group information office;
8. an increase in the scope and depth of information in the annual report and accounts together with other financial statements.

Are visible signs of the growing appreciation of the importance of financial communications by the corporate sector.

Company Survey on the Role and Benefits of Financial Public Relations

Interviews with a number of major companies undertaken in 1982 and 1983 on the perceived role and benefits of financial public relations yielded a number of interesting and diverse views on the nature of financial public relation.

> "It helps create an accurate analysis of what the group is doing. It helps maintain goodwill in the investing communities. It possibly smooths share price fluctuations which arise from speculation and rumour. It may make it cheaper to raise money if people have confidence in the share price. The role of Unilever investor relations activity is, by providing clarification and explanation, to help those interested in Unilever to make the best use of publicly available information, to stop them making obvious factual errors, to explain how economic forces interact with our type of business and to help them nraw sensible inferences from these facts. The quality press base thier piece on us from us and conversations with investment analysts who follow Unilever. This is the main source for their profit forecasts.

Market forces will more the market up and down but the position of the company within that movement will be condition by the knowledge and understanding of the company. It is the accuracy of the information which may cause a rise in price or a fall but it your communication is good your price will always be better than it would otherwise have have been.

If creates a better understanding of business realities and performance of the company.

If we did it, it would bring a greater awareness!

It creates a better understanding by the financial community but this is achieved principally through regular contact with investment analysts.

To be better known is good for conducting business, it oils the wheels of business if you are well known and have a good reputation and it makes business life easier.

The financial community, if they understand you, are more likely to be sympathetic to what you want to do.

Financial advertising and financial PR are complementary, but you can't beat a face-to-face chat with institutional investors and their advisors.

To ensure that the audience to which your communication is addressed is fully informed of the company's activities, objectives and business philosophy.

It oils the wheels of borrowing and of buying and selling companies.

The aim of PR is to lay the long-term foundations for the next rights issue.

It doesn't help a company if the investing public is taken by surprise. I am trying to ensure that no one is taken by surprise.

Reasons for Adopting Financial PR

Iterviews with a number of companies brought to attention a diversity of factors.

Financial PR began at our company as a need to service the information seeking inquiries that came from the media and stockbrokers.

In the early 1970s we discovered we had a fuddy-duddy image in the City. For our development and diversification it became important to create the right image. We needed the help of the financial community to achieve our objectives in acquisitions and finance to support our expansion.

It cannot be in a company's best interest for people not to be make an informed judgement. It's in a company's interest, especially a responsible company, and in the best interest be in a position to make a valid judgement relating to all factors.

We have taken account of the shift in shareholder profile and supply increasingly sophisticated information in our accounts.

To build mutual understanding between ourselves and the City.

To maintain a favourable image of company with City institutions and the general public.

We began with outside PR in 1967, It provides external confidential advice. It extends the company's in-house PR facilities especially with respect to City contacts.

One company, which appointed its first in-house financial public relations executive as late as 1981, explained the muti-causal factors in his appointment:

We had our quotation and loyal shareholders; there was little trade in our share and not much interest in them. We were self-financing so that there was no need for City contact. Then some directors relised that it was not good practice to avoid the City. Our share price was poor, only one quarter of the market average for our sector and this wasn't good for morale. A decision was taken to build a bridge to the City and two of the directors went out to meet brokers and their institutional clients. We discovered that our company had no image at all. The City was totally ignorant of our diversification into paper, packaging, cosmetics and engineering. Our huge pre-tax profit was beyond City comprehension, there's only one place in the world that understands such figures—the Texas oil industry. So we explained our high level of profit. We established a broker-analyst relationship because nowadays everyone goes to the brokers for the instant quote.

Factors in the Growth of Financial PR

The expansion in financial communications has a number of different causes, of which the most significant have been 'push' factors. Of these, most important and long term in operation are regulatory factors including changes in company law, Stock regulations, the establishment of the Takeover Panel and changes in accounting practice. Recent Companies Acts have required greater disclosure of financial information by all public companies. The Companies Act of 1967, as we have already seen, represents a milestone in company disclosure. The Companies Act of 1981, whose principal objective was to introduce the requirements of the EEC's Fourth Directive, also obliges companies to provide fuller information about their activities in the directors' report. In the future, a new Companies Act will probably expand the information required to be supplied to employees. Statutes have been a principal force in widening and deepening the information that companies make public and consequently expanding financial public relations activity. Likewise, the activities of the Stock Exchange Council in tightening up its quotation requirements and conditions for new issues have moved companies in the same direction, whilst the Takeover Panel regulates for certain disclosures during bid battles. More significantly, the vulnerability of the majority of British companies to takeover bids has had a great impact. The rise in takeovers since the 1960s has driven home to many companies the importance of maintaining good relations with shareholders. Those companies engaged in bid struggles have recognised the need to put their case forward and have employed financial public relations experts to help them do it. Subordinate to them is the role of the accountancy profession. The rapid rise in the number of certified and chartered accountants, from 29,300 in 1956 to 100,535 in 1982-3, has supplied big business not only with more financial information than ever before but has also established new and complex accounting procedures. It is the increasing complexity of company figures, combined with financial journalists' misunderstanding of them, that has persuaded many companies of the need to explain their financial results.

The adoption of shareholder relations from the late 1950s also ownes much to the political wish to encourage a capital-owning democracy, successor to the nineteenth-century Liberal cry for 'two acres and a cow'. Individual companies such as De la Rue under the chairmanship of Bernard Westall, ICI under Paul Chambers, Rugby Portland Cement under Halford Reddish were very active in promoting shareholder relations. The influence of the Wider Share Ownership Movement, the spread of employee participation schemes and the growth in numbers of private shareholders were instrumental in the adoption of financial public relations by the corporate sector. In addition, popular financial journalism spawned by the revival of the unit trust industry and growing advertising revenues from the promotion of financial products created opportunities for financial public relations activity.

There are also a variety of short-term causal factors. For some companies, the adoption of financial public relations was a defensive reaction. For example, the banks' adoption of a joint industry public relations campaign in 1974 was the response to the threat of nationalisation. The campaign to explain their huge profits was another consequence. Other factors were also important, such as the realisation of their poor public image and, for some, the exposure of their heavy involvement in politically sensitive areas. For other companies, it was peer group pressure—responding to rivals' innovations—that caused wide-scale adoption of financial public relations. For particuiar company sectors other pressures were at work. For some it was a response to ecology to environmental and consumerist lobbies. There are also more broad and longer-lasting factors such as the adoption of marketing, the recognition of the wider social and economic resgonsibilities of the company sector and the apprecition that a well-informed press is in the long run move valuable than a good write-up.

Finally, there are three economic and financial factors. The economic upheavals of 1973-74, including the rise in oil prices, the secondary banking crisis, the share price collapse and the slow-down in world trade, caused not only economic and financial difficulties for many companies but resulted in a strategic reappraisal of the company's activities combined with a management restructuring and changes at board level. These factors contributed to the increasing adoption of financial public relations from the mind-1970s. Companies in financial difficulties, as well as companies facing changed economic circumstances, found it necessary to explain themselves to the shareholders and the press. Largely unaccustomed to explaining themselves to anybody, they sought the advice of financial public relations experts. Also significant was the share price fall which concentrated managers' minds on the value of their share price in the market, compared with their estimation of what their estimation of what it should be. In many cases, the adoption of financial public relations secured a readjustment and re-rating. Their experiences since that time have reinforced the trends towards increased disclosure, and to tailoring the message with the help of financial PR. Another major factor has been the increased reliance on medium to long-term finance from the banks. The banks, chiefly the clearing banks, have taken an increased interest in lending to the corporate sector. In 1972 lenders were primarily interested in a company's cash position in order to provide a rolling overdraft. With the change to long-term loans of between five and eight years, the banks have become interested in cash flows and this means they have got closer to the heart of a company's position. Bank loans became increasingly important to companies during the 1970s. A recent survey by the Bank of England of 1,200 industrial and commercial companies found that, between 1967 and 1982, the proportion of bank borrowings in companies' total indebtedness nose from 30 to 80 per cent.[17]

But perhaps the most significant factor of all in the adoption of financial communications and financial public relations is the rise to dominance of the institutional investor (see table 8.1). In

1957, private individuals held 65 per cent of ordinary share capital; by 1982 their share had fallen to between 25 and 30 per cent. Institutional investors now at least 70 per cent of the ordinary share capital of UK companies traded on the Stock Exchange. This profound change in the investment profile is reflected in significant changes at company level. For example, between 1970 and 1980, BOC found its institutional shareholding rise from 44 to 75 per cent of its ordinary share capital; RTZ's rose from 58.6 to 75 per cent in the same period. Between 1971 and 1980 Unilever saw the institutions' share of its ordinary share capital rise from 30 to 60 per cent. In 1981 institutional investors accounted for 72 per cent of ICI's equity; in 1979 institutions accounted for 77 per cent of Tube Investments ordinary share capital. As companies saw an increasing proportion of their equity concentrated in the hands of a small number of powerful investors, they recognised the need and opportunity for increased communications, set up investor relation programmes and adopted full-scale financial public relations. Not only was it important for companies to talk to their institutional investors; increasingly, fund managers liked to meet the management of companies they had invested in. The City lunch between institutional investors and top management of a company (the chairman and finance director), organised by the company's stockbroker, is an opportunity for both sides to meet face to face to supplement hard financial data with other inputs. It is possible for companies at such an occasion to talk directly with 30 per cent of their entire equity shareholding. Such contacts are made all the more necessary by the change in investment habits of the institutions. According to the Wilson Committee Report, the investing institutions have, since 1963, become active traders in ordinary share. Up to 1967, insurance companies and pension found invesments in equities were long term (over twenty years); by 1973-77 the length of their investments had fallen to eight and six years respectively.[18] Moreover, before 1973 it was rnre for persion funds to measure their performance. The All-Share Index only became available in 1973 and it is only since that time that some stookbroking firms and consulting actuaries have developed

TABLE 12.1

Beneficial Ownership of Listed UK Ordinary Shares, 1957-81

Category of Beneficial Shareholders	*Per cent of Total Shareholdings at Market Value*				
	1957	*1963*	*1969*	*1975*	*1981*
Persons	65.8	54.0	47.4	37.5	28.2
Charities and other non-profit-making bodies serving persons	1.9	2.1	2.1	2.3	2.2
Stockbrokers and jobbers	0.9	1.4	7.4	0,4	—
Banks	0.9	1.3	1.7	0.7	0.3
Insurance companies	8.8	10.0	12.2	15.9	20.5
Pension funds	3.4	6.4	9.0	16.8	26.7
Investment trust companies and other financial companies	6.8	10.0	8.7	10.1	6.8
Units trusts	0.5	1.3	2.9	4.1	3.6
Industrial and commercial companies	2.7	5.1	5.4	3.0	5.1
Public sector	3.9	1.5	2.6	3.6	3.0
Overseas sector	4.4	7.0	6.6	5.6	3.6
Total	100.0	100.0	100 0	100.0	100.0

Sources: Committee to Review the Functioning of Financial Institutions, Cmnd 7937, HMSO, 1988, p. 500 and the Stock Exchange.

computer programmes to measure performance. Today, they produce a regular acturial analysis of investment performance for institutional clients, which has led to the development of the 'beauty contest' where trustees ask fund managers to make presentations— a new aspect of financial promotion. It has also meant that City institutions are expected to be more professional. The ability to measure performance, the need to meet short-term performance targets and the change in investment philosophy of institutional investors have combined to keep companies on their toes. To keep their institutional investors satisfied, companies must perform satisfactorily, and keep their shareholders well informed.

The increase in importance of the institutional investor over the last 25 years is one strand in the companies' changed attitudes towards shareholder relations and the adoption of financial PR. Another strand is that the dominance of institutional investors has caused a change in the broking function. Instead of individual private clients, brokers now have a long list of institutional clients, for whom they compete on the quality of their reseasch output. Thus broker analysts have increased in number from 250 in 1,200 in 1970 and 2,000 in 1982. It is the broker analyst's function to make an investment appraisal of a company, forecast its profits and to advise clients to buy, sell or hold. In order to fulfil this function analysts have demanded more and more information from companies. For their part, companies have responded with an increase in the number of press releases, an increased depth and scope of financial data presented in financial statements, invitations for site visits, and a willingness to inform directly on any event of importance to shareholders, such as acquisitions, divestments, rumours, board changes, and a change in debt profile or company structure. Companies today issue a stream of information, tailored by public relations to the financial community and the press. Not only have such communications increased but their quality has improved. As one former 'Lex' put it:

In the 1960s the average big company would talk to The Times, the Financial Times and occasionally the Telegraph over a cup of tea and that would be that.

Today, companies talk to financial journalists and the City over lunch, press briefings, presentations and the telephone. Company attitudes towards the media have undergone a revolution. In the early stages of financial public relations, editorial comment became more informed on the basis of the greater flow of information from companies. Then, at some point in the 1970s, willingness to supply information, in the hope of informed comment, became allied to need. The market place was changing rapidly, and financial accounts were becoming too complex; consequently it became necessary for companies to present their information in a more easily assimilable style with lots of background information so that the report in the press, when it came, was accurate, The search for accuracy and understanding, both by the media and the City, has become a major force in the adoption of financial public relations.

The change in the corporate sector's attitude towards the press and the City was, as we have seen, the result of a variety of interrelated thrusts. Subordinate to these were the attractions and opportunities offered by full-scale financial public relations. Most seductive of all was the promise of editorial mention, not only in the form of favourable special articles but the PR-inspired topical discussion in the press, and on radio and television. Allied to this was the wish of companies to avoid misrepresentation by the media. Another, and no less important, factor was the recognition of what financial public relations could achieve for a company's investment rating and share price. It became the aim of many companies to provide financial advisers and investors with the information necessary to assess the true value of shares. A process of education and information was seen as the means to achieve this aim. Some of the more spectacular achievements in this field, which were widely quoted in the press, no doubt stimulated more companies in this area. One such example was that of BOC, mentioned in The Times on 18 July 1982. BOC had embarked upon a corporate communications programme, aimed at the financial community, in order to elevate its presence and change its imago from 'an overpriced, boring industrial group that could not make money to a progressive, enterprising and dynamic company'.[19] A survey showed that as a result the proportion of brokers recommending 'buy BOC' rose from 17 per cent in 1979 to 26 per cent in 1981 and the share price rose from 56p at the end of 1979 to 161p in July 1982.

Additional advantages from PR activities in the City, which had not escaped senior management, included the amity of City allies in future capital raising operations, takeover bids and mergers. Indeed corporate finance advisers now recommend retaining financial PR companies to execute part of their defensive/offensive strategies for companies. Lastly the press abounded with examples of good and bad public relations. One recent casualty was the John Brown engineering firm which received a critical press in 1981-82, highlighting the disadvantages and repercussions of misinforming the City with its wildly optimistic profit forecast and ill-conceived rights issue. More recently, the press and City have shown their appreciation at being kept well informed. The Lex column noted:

> Thorn EMI had put up such conspicuous signposts to a poor half-year performance that the market took to a 39 per cent downturn in pre-tax profits—to £27.6m—yesterday as though it was manna from heaven. The shares moved up 22p, helped by the group's forecast of a recovery in the current half.[20]

Such examples have served as a constant reminder to companies to cultivate good relations with both the press and the financial community.

The Principal Techniques

The annoucement of financial results is a major component of a company's financial public relations activity. In the post-war years, for most companies, the posting of the annual report and accounts has superseded the annual general meeting, and growing more important as the focus of interest to shareholders and the press is the preliminary announcement. The accounts have themselves become a public relations vehicle and, the day they are released, give rise to a great deal of public relations activity. Many companies use the occasion to hold a press conference for financial and trade journalists at which members of the board give a short presentation and answer journalists' questions. Similarly, the other object of a company's attentions, the investment analyst, is catered for by individual briefings from the company or a conference. All interested parties are usually supplied with fact sheets or background notes in which the management presents its views. In addition, senior management and the public relations department are usually available to answer questions by telephone. One company's financial public relations officer observed that, at the last financial results announcement, he had spent six hours on the telephone and had spoken to nine analysts and five journalists.

In spite of the electronic revolution, the press release remains the principal means of communicating a company's financial announcements to the press. It reaches the desks of financial journalists very quickly, usually one hour after the announcement on the Stock Exchange. For many large companies, the press conference is today no less important than before. However, financial public relations activity has established close relationships between companies and financial and trade journalists. Such links once established and nurtured by the occasional lunch and more frequent telephone conversations have led to the recognition that a telephone conversation at this time can be a useful alternative. In addition, some companies have recognised the shift in press and City interest to the announcement of preliminary results and have responded to this by shifting the press conference to that day. In the future it is most likely that we shall see a shift of public relations activity to the announcement of preliminary results in order to obtain more informed editional comment when press interest is at its greatest.

The announcement of interim results is also an event of importance. The backbone to this, as in the case of other announcements, is the press release distributed by the City advertising agency or, on accasion, by in-house facilities. It is also an opportunity for the stockbroker/fund manager/company lunch.

The City lunch has grown in importance and frequency, in parallel with the growth in importance of institutional investors in a company's shareholder profile. Post-war private shareholders were the owners of relatively small numbers of shares; they were traditionally numerous and inaccessible beyond the customary advertisements, notification of dividend and annual report and accounts. But, more significantly, the private shareholder was a long-term investor, traditionally loyal to the board inspite of his tenuous links with the company. The new investors—the financial institutions—had, by contrast, large holdings and, as a group, accounted for an increasing proportion of the ordinary share capital. Moreover they were relatively small in number and therefore more accessible. Their accessibility and their large holdings provided the key to serious investor relations. More significantly, as time went by, the institutions' increasing tendency to invest short term compelled companies to communicate more frequently. Thus turnover by the investing institutions accounted for almost 40 per cent of Stock Exchange turnover in 1965 and rose to over 60 per cent In 1979.[21] Accessibility and large holdings were crucial for company communications directed at the institutional investor. The City lunch became the formalised institution of such relations. The largest British companies are known to have as many as ten such lunches a year arranged by their official stockbroker with a section of fund managers. Smaller companies may have only two such meetings a year. The lunch is attended by the chairman and senior financial personnel who give a short presentation covering the current trading position followed by an extensive question and answer session. The lunch is the principal means of communicating with major investors, or, as one financial in house PR man said: to keep them advised and make them feel comfortable with their investment in us, and to create the right sort of image'. The City lunch is therefore a very important and serious event. It has resulted in a change in the share price on the same afternoon. For example, according to Lex, severe falls in the price of ICI and Cadbury Schweppes shares followed one such lunch.[22]

The increasing focus on the City is one of the post-war themes of financial public relations. Financial PR has provided the basis for broker forecasts of profits; the basis of the brokers' recommendations to buy/hold/sell. It has achieved a market re-rating of company shares. However, one factor may now be upsetting this flow of information from companies to the City and reducing the company's ability to explain itself. It is the insider-dealing provisions of the Companies Act of 1980 which came into force on 23 June 1980. As The Times commented with respect to the John Brown affair:

> One [consequence] is that some of the old channels of communication between the City and industry have been blocked by the law on insider dealing. The nudges that investment analysts would have had from finance directors over trading prospects and profit forecasts have become a lot less direct.[23]

Moreover, at the beginning of 1983. several broker forecasts proved hopelessly wrong, so much so as to encourage Lex to ask:

> Are the numbers getting more complicated or are the rules on insider information weakening the city's teaditional flow of well-informed news?[24]

The periodic announcements of financial results represent a crescendo in the activities of a company's financial public relations activity. However financial public relations is in effect a continuous process. often a day-to-day activity. In house financial public relations personnel and senior finance personnel are readily available to the journalist, stockbroker and investment analyst. Companies sustain contact with stockbrokers throughout. Each company will direct its efforts to a group of stockbrokers and analysts known to be especially interested in their sector, The mining eompanies concentrate on 25-40 stock-broking firms serious'y interested in the mining sector; insurance companies concentrate on the two dozen stockbroking firms that follow the composite insurance sector; Unilever concentrates on the twenty investment analysts who follow them in detail. ICI likewise concentrates on the 30 who watch ICI, while the energy-based companies concentrate on the 30-40 dealing mainly in the energy sector. Analysts are briefed, invited for lunch and taken on site visits. Contact by telephone is frequent. Any factor that is likely to affect the prott and loss account or the balance sheet has to be announced under Stock Exchange regulations. Acquisitions, disposals, any change in the debt profile, company structure, board changes, adoption of new technology give rise to communications. Such events will be relayed to the City. Nor is it a one-way traffic. Most investment analysts now send a draft of their circular to companies giving them the opportunity to correct any factual errors, since such circulars form a major factor in the institutions' investment decisions. Contacts between the company and the investment analyst are therefore frequent and occur at any time in the year. It is only during the month or so ahead of the announcement of company results that a company's conversations with analysts and the press are highly restricted in range. This is partly the consequence of the insider-information rules, and partly it is a customary truce.

Finally, emerging in the 1970s and still not particularly widespread, is a change in attitude by companies towards the communication of financial results to their employees. Some companies have recognised the value of keeping employees well informed on their finance status and progress and have created positive communication channels. The special employee report, the equivalent of the annual report and accounts in a simplified form, a 1950s innovation by Halford Reddish, chairman of Rugby Portland Cement, has been adopted by a number of companies including Marks and Spencer and the BOC group early on. BOC began to produce emloyee reports at the beginning of the 1970s. However, they discovered that their employees were more interested in the status and progress of their particular factory or subsidiary than in the status of the group as a whole. These findings caused them to abandon employee reports in favour of newsletters specific to each plant or subsidiary. Information at local level was provided to each group of employees. Alternatively, some companies automatically supply their employees with a copy of the annual report and accounts whilst others will only respond to a request for a copy. House journals are anotner means of communicating financial results to employees and it is probable that this remains the main medium of communication. A small number of companies have adopted newmedia to communicate with employees at all levels and transmit annual financial results by video or audiovisual presentations, while a handful of companies such as Whitbread, Blue Circle, Marks and Spencer, Associatad Biscuits and Calor Group, have used special films as a medium to communicate annual results to employees.[25] However, on the whole, staff communications are a relatively underdeveloped area in Britain, reflecting poor industrial relations and a distinct separation of management from other levels. As recently as 1981, Lord Sieff, chairman of Marks and Spencer said:

> There is very little that needs to be kept secret. . . . The great majority of emplôyees appreciate being taken into the confidence of top management, but regrettably mueh top management still believes in telling employees as little as possible of what is happening instead of as much as possible.[26]

The state of company-employee communications is so poor that a new clause was added to the Employment Bill of 1982 to secure from companies 'an awareness by all employees of the financial and economic factors affecting the performance of the company,'[27] and a future Companies Act will include far-reaching provisions, including one that a company's actions must take into account the best interests of the staff. Therefore, while financial PR in the 1970s was largely externally orientated, statutory changes will ensure a greater internal orientation of finaucial PR. The impact of financial PR will broaden and deepen and be of even greater significance in the 1980s.

We have now dealt with the communication of financial results by the corporate sector and the techniques used to distribute information. We have seen that financial public relations grew out of the need to have someone in the company to organise the interface with the media and the brokers. Whilst the stockbrokers and the press are not in themselves investors, they are a link between the company and its shareholders. We have examined the reasons for adoption of in-house financial public relations personnel and observed that the company's progress and financiai status are the chief subject matter of financial public relations. Economic and financial circumstances change so quickly that officially required financial statements that lie six months apart have to be supplemented by a continuous flow of information in order to ensure that shareholders are as fully informed as possible. And it is through the independent media and City stockbrokers that the majority of investors are more fully informed than ever before.

The Services Provided by the Financial PR Agency and Consultancy

The services offered by the financial public relations agency to the corporate sector fail into two broad groups. Historically, first and still important are the mechanical tasks, including the distribution of company press releases and, more recently, a same-day direct mailing service for companies to institutional brokers. Another task is arranging the press conference and ensuring that the journalists invited are interested in the company's sector. The monitornig of analysts' and journalists' specialisms and acting as door openers to financial and trade journalists as well as city analysts is yet another. In addition, an outside financial public relations specialist would, when called upon, help draft the press release or background notes, anticipate journalists' questions and focus the message according to its final destination. Other areas of work that have grown up are miscellaneous, including the commissioning of a variety of research projects, and establishing corporate communications objectives. Sometimes, research provides the angle in product promotion. For example, Legal and General's 'What is a housewife worth?' campaign in promoting insurance for wives was based on research findings and achieved enormous amounts of free publicity. Whatever the combination of techniques employed, financial public relations activity reinforces the 'above the line' promotions conducted by West End agencies for the corporate sector.

A more recent and significant development has been the development of a strategic advisory and executive capacity which is increasingly employed in a variety of areas, including corporate communications, the communications of financial information to employees, shareholder relations, communications during takeover bids and new issues. The financial PR man has grown up with the introduction of professional management into the upper reaches of UK companies and the adoption of American business techniques. The outside financial PR consultant is brought in either to evolve the communications strategy suited to corporate objectives (defined by the company) or to execute corporate communications. This, in a way, is the follow-on from calling in American management consultants such as McKinsey and others. Perhaps the crucial value of an outside financial public relations firm is the offering of advice based on experience; in essence, it is 'knowing when not to do things'; it is presenting the right measage in the right place at the right time to a variety of audiences, includidg the City and the press. The communication effectiveness of outside PR consultancies with the press has been the subject of market research conducted by MORI. Although the question is subjective, it is, nevertheless, the only piece of unbiased research available. The results of the poll of 30 journalists who were asked 'How effective overall would you say the following agencies are in their relationship with the press? is shown in table 12.2.

TABLE 12.2

Extract from Market and Opinion Research International's 1981-82 Annual Survey (per cent)

	Very/fairly effective	*Not very/ not at all effective*	*Donot know*
Dewe Rogerson	97	—	3
Streets Financial	87	13	—
Charles Barker Lyons	73	23	3
Extel PR	73	23	3
Shandwick Consultants	73	17	10
CIPS (St. James's)	70	20	10
Good Relations City	63	27	10
Burson-Marsteller	67	30	13
Nathan PR	57	20	23
Shareholder Relations	53	27	20
Carl Byoir	40	37	23
Good Relations Group	40	30	30
Daniel J. Edelman	37	37	27
Hill and Knowlton	37	43	20
Lexington International	30	37	33
Kingsway	10	40	50
FTB	7	50	43
Gwynne-Hart	3	27	70

Since the 1960s, the role of corporate financial public relations has broadened and deepened. Financial public relations has become an essential element in other spheres of business life; the takeover battle, new issues and image-building exercises.

The announcement of financial results has been supplemented by day-to-day activity; the company provides a continuous stream of information on the one hand and, on the other, company personnel are constantly available to financial journalists and City interests. New media have been employed, including radio, television and the international news service. The traditional view that financial public relations was the supplying of information primarily to a financial audience has been succeeded by the modern view that there are many audiences; employees, customers, suppliers, the government and the public. The modern corporation faces a multiple audience with multiple interests and reactions for whom information must not only be available but must be tailored for each audience and explanations given at a variety of levels. The provision of explanation has become a cornerstone of corporate communications.

In the new issue field there is in a sense a perversity in the direction of financial public relations activity. The 1950s and 1960s were dominated by mass communications techniques suited to the widening of private share ownership; the 1970s were characterised by financial public relations employing very particular public relations techniques aimed at a narrow and small target audienee, perhaps as few as 600 institutional investors and their advisers representing 70 per cent of the ordinary equity. The early 1980s have seen a tendency to promote wider private share ownership under the government's privatisation drive, requiring a return to mass communication to reach 'the man in the street'.

In the future it will become necessary for financial pubilc relations to improve their execution of corporate communications; to transmit a broader information flow to opinion formers and City interests, to drive home the unique factors determining a company's status and prospects including the structure and composition of the business, its geogrraphic spread and product diversification, as well as such general factors as the importance of currency movements to final results.

Only in this way will clearer perspectives of the business entity be attained.

VERBAL COMMUNICATION—ITS SCIENTIFIC BASIS IN NLP*

Synopsis: Just 50 words are used for almost two-third of the social conversation of the average adult (when not trying to impress)—so state scientific studies carried out in the U.S.A. of the process of normal/spontaneous conversation. The synergistic aid of one-way mirrors, telescopes and long-range microphones, high speed video cameras and recorders, minicomputers. etc. permit scientists unobtrusively to observe, study and analyse both the Oral and 'Body-English' forms of human communication. This article describes a new scientific principle, called 'Neurolinguistic programming' (NLP). NLP explains the scientific rationale for several individually known manifestations of behaviour. Additionally, it helps us to make several important deductions about 'what the other person is really saying'.

Management scientists have so far defined six categories of oral communication and Body-English as relevant for business purposes. Five of them are briefly given below, partly as an aidememoire, partly to provide an appropriate background for the proper understanding of NLP, which is the subject of this article.

1. Linguistics: Words and the rules governing the order in which they are used. (Grammar, syntax, etc.)
2. Paralinguistics: One kind consists of sounds other than words *e.g.* "Ha! Ha!". "Tsk Tsk!" The other consists of the tone and expression of the voice, including emphasis when using words. Tone and expression mainly come

*By P.G. Menon.

from the vowel sounds, which are generally controlled by the Right Hemisphere of the Cerebral Cortex (the top part of the brain) except, apparently, in the case of Japanese.

3. Kinesics : Body-movements that convey a message (He approached the Boss confidently), and expressions, particularly of the face. The eyebrows alone have 23 possible positions/expressions, according to R. Birdwhistell, the 'father' of modern Kinesics. However, Indian Management-trainers should note tnat respected Western experts are coming to learn from our desi Kinesics experts, in classical Indian dance.
4. Haptics : Touching. This is not to be confused with the 'verbal storking' of Transactional Analysis. Nor does it encompass 'laying on of hands', management-theorists, including those in HRD (human resources development) prefer to skirt spiritual issues. (The only normal reference is to "self-actualisation" in Maslow's theory of Motivation.) Nor does haptics cover the process of receiving information by the person who touches. This form of passive communication is the province of Medicine. However, modern medico-scientific instruments that can detect and record brain-waves reveal that many so-called 'executive gut feelings' are actually intellectual, not emotional, in nature, because they are the non-verabal communication of the Right brain—it is the left hemisphere that is verbal. Incidentally, the USSR is computerising the haptics knowledge of Indian experts, such as the nature of the communication from the human pulse that the Ayurvedic physician records when he uses the 3-finger method of pulse-taking.
5. Proxemics : From the work of the Anthropologist E. Hall. It deals with Body Orientation (*e.g.* : "He turned his back on me."), and with the meaning of the space a person keeps between himself and others (*e.g.* : "He was also very distant with me.").

According to American researchers on human communications, the Linguistic mode may convey as little as 7% of the message (which is why a limited variety of words is used); the Paralinguistic modes convey another 25% (this is why people find a 'dead' or 'flat' tone of voice unattractive); Kinesics 50% to 55% Haptics and Proxemics provide the remaining 13% to 18%. This explains why some people are very uncomfortable if they have to conduct serious conversations over the telephone. They find it very difficult to compensate for the loss all except the Linguistic and Paralinguistic modes. You will recall that these two account for only a third of normal communication. The American adnlt, when speaking English, uses in all about 2,000 words. But nearly two-third of his meaning comes from just 50 words such as : "I, you, the. a, not, just, is, are, can, say, thing, get, have . . . .'. Futhermore, 500 of the commonly-used words in English have about 14,000 meanings. So, the problem becomes even more difficult when the communication mode is restricted to the most limited of all modes : the purely Linguistic, *i.e.* to the written word only. Learning to write is a tedious process that takes years of application. That is why, in every Bureaucracy, now and in the past, the passport to succees was mastery over the written word, not leadership or other inter-personal aptitudes. It is therefore important for studies to be carried out in India about the range of words in telephonic business conversation and the extent to which the words do not compensate for the loss of the other modes. It is well-known that many bureaucrats and executives will, if they have the power, insist on a face-to-face meeting for the purpose of 'clarification', even if letters have already been written. It is often assumed by the 'victims', *i.e.*, by those who have to go for the tete a tete, that the other is merely tying to avoid having to commit to paper. This may be true in fewer cases than is commonly supposed. The true cause may lie in the area of NLP. NLP has some entirely new dimensions to offer; it also enriches our understanding of the Linguistic, Kinesics and Haptics and permits us to use the latter two in a verbal way.

What is Neurolinguistic Programming ?

The term sounds odd to the layman, because it comes from the medical sciences, NLP is based on the fact that we experience the world through our senses : eyes, ears, 'sense of touch', etc. The data received through each sense is stored in a part of the brain different for each sense. This neurophysical base is the same for all Mankind. Hence NLP provides a set of common and unique guidelines, unlike 'body-English', which is not a Lingua Franca (yes, that was meant to be punny), and which can deliberately be faked.

We experience the world through our senses. The eyes, ears and the surface of the body receive per second about 100,000 butes/inputs, which are coded and transmitted electrically to the brain, where they are decoded, filtered, stored, retrieved, processed. NLP is concerned only with the Auditory, Kinesthetic and Visual modes. It ignores Taste and Smell, which the brain receives in the form of chemical signals.

The eye is, actually, an extension of the brain, not a separate organ connected to the brain. Hence the position of the eyes indicates from which of the three stores (A, K or V) data/information is being retrieved or beidg processed. Hence NLP deciphers the real 'language of the eyes', deciphers its apparently meaningless movements. What will you see if you look at the eyes of a normal right-handed person facing you and either talking to you or responding to your interrogation ? Table 12.3 tells you.

Please note that the process is reversed in the case of the left-handed. Another point of relevance to those wondering whether to make a deeper study of NLP is that data from the right half of each eye goes to the Left brain and that from the left half of each eye to the Right brain. So the V-mode position of the eyes is in accordance with our knowledge from other sources that 'programme' (in EDP jargon) are handled by the Left brain.

TABLE 12.3

Position of Eyes From Your View-Point	*What It means*
At 2 O'clock	Visual memory
At 3 O'clock	Auditory memory
At 5 O'clock	Auditory, probably an internal dialogue.
At 7 O'clock	Kinesthetic, including internal sensations such as emotions and the purely intellectual response of the Right brain as translated into the K mode.
At 9 O'clock	Auditory construction (imagining yourself doing something you have never done before).
At 11 O'clock	Visual construction.
Looking straight ahead, but unfocused	Visual, either memory or construction.

We have all noticed that the eyes wander, or go vague, of people from whom you least expect such behaviour, people who are obviously listening intently to you or as intentity trying to communicate to you, Their inattention is only apparent. These eye-movements show those familiar with NLP that the person has gone into himself', either to consult his mental records (*i.e.*, 'retrieve from Store'), or to imagine a new 'happening', or to hold an internal dialogue with himself. Your role at this stage is to decide whether to interrupt his train of thought, whether to remain quiet and observe, or whether to encourage the flow of his thought.

Using NLP Words

When doing any of the above, the extent of your rapport with the other person will depend on the extent to which you match your channels of communication with those the other person is using. 'Matching' means mirroring, *i.e.*, copying those channels. That is, in TA terms you should be in the appropriate Ego-States; in terms of Dr. Kahler's increasingly-popular Process-Communication Model you should one of the three channels called The Computer, The Comforter, or The Emoter, But, most important of all are the NLP words, and phrases. This is the seeond theoretical concept of NLP, the first being the eye-position, and its basis is as follows : Your verbal description of any experience, real or imagined, is nothing but a reproduction/representation of the original experience. So your description uses words relevant to lhe NLP mode through which the input was received. Consider this statement : I understand what you mean." :—

A primarily auditory person will say : That sounds clear to me".

A primarily Kinesthetic person will say : I grasp your meaning".

A primarily visual person will say : "I see what you mean".

This scientifically proven fact permits you to identify the category that anyone favours most, by listening to him, and noting what NLP words he most uses. These will be verbs, adjectives and adverbs.

Auditory expressions include : gamut of emotions, harmonious relations, discordant, comes in loud and clear, rings a bell, sound him out.

Kinesthetic : apprehend, bring to my notice, caught my eye, chilling reply, concrete proposal, feels right, I'll handle that, palpable, press him to do it, a rough draft, tangible, in touch with, weight the idea, let us wrap up this part of the discussion.

Visual : appears to be, bright idea, clarify coloured his outlook, focus attention, it came in a flash, the chances look good reflects the true picture, very perceptive, see my meaning ?